I HAVE NO GUN
BUT I CAN SPIT

I HAVE NO GUN
BUT I CAN SPIT

an anthology of satirical and abusive verse
selected by

KENNETH BAKER

EYRE METHUEN LONDON

First published in 1980 by Eyre Methuen Ltd
11 New Fetter Lane, London EC4P 4EE
Reprinted 1980

This anthology © 1980 by Kenneth Baker

Individual poems ©
as indicated in Acknowledgements

British Library Cataloguing in Publication Data

I have no gun but I can spit.
1. Satire, English   2. English poetry
I. Baker, Kenneth
821'.07   PR1195.S3

ISBN 0-413-47500-X

Filmset, printed and bound in Great Britain by
Hazell Watson & Viney Ltd, Aylesbury, Bucks

CONTENTS

England Of Cant And Smug Discretion

And Hate My Next-Door Neighbour

Let The Day Perish Wherein I Was Born

The Wicked Grocer Groces . . .

We Thought At First, This Man Is A King For Sure

War's A Brain-Spattering, Windpipe-Slitting Art

Come Let Us Mock At The Great

O Age Without A Soul

He Is The Pinprick Master

ACKNOWLEDGEMENTS

The editor and publishers are very grateful to Professor Edward Mendelson for permission to use part of the postscript of W. H. Auden's *The Birth of Architecture* as the title of this anthology and wish to thank the following poets, poets' executors and estates, publishers and literary agents for permission to reproduce poems and extracts from poems as listed below:

Kingsley Amis for a poem from *Collected Poems 1944-1979* © 1978 Kingsley Amis;

Faber and Faber Ltd and Random House Inc. for one complete poem and an extract from a poem by W. H. Auden from *Collected Poems*;

Leonard Barras for two poems from *Hailstones On Your Father* (Iron Press);

Elizabeth Bartlett for two poems from *A Lifetime Of Dying* (Harry Chambers/Peterloo Poets, 1979 available (1980) price £1.95 post free from Treovis Farm Cottage, Upton Cross, Liskeard, Cornwall);

Mrs J. C. Baxter for a poem by James K. Baxter;

The Estate of Max Beerbohm for three poems from *Max In Verse* (William Heinemann);

A. D. Peters & Co Ltd for three poems by Hilaire Belloc from *Complete Verse* (Gerald Duckworth);

John Betjeman for three poems from *Collected Poems* (John Murray);

Edward Bond for two poems from *Theatre Poems and Songs* (Eyre Methuen);

Howard Brenton for a poem previously published in the *New Statesman*;

John Baker Publishers Ltd for a poem by Pennethorne Hughes from *38 Poems By Pennethorne Hughes* (John Baker, 1970);

The National Trust for three poems by Rudyard Kipling from *Collected Poems* (Macmillan);

Tom Lehrer for a lyric from *The Tom Lehrer Song Book* (Paul Elek, 1953);

Bernard Levin for a poem first published in *The Times*;

Mr Omar S. Pound for two poems by Wyndham Lewis first published in *Blast* © The Estate of the late Mrs G. A. Wyndham Lewis;

Christopher Logue for two poems © 1969 and 1980 by Christopher Logue;

Mrs Valda Grieve for five poems and an extract from a poem by Hugh MacDiarmid from *The Complete Poems of Hugh MacDiarmid* (Martin Brian & O'Keeffe);

Faber and Faber Ltd for two poems by Louis MacNeice from *The Collected Poems of Louis MacNeice*;

The Literary Trustees of Walter de la Mare and The Society of Authors as their representative for a poem first published in *Blast*;

Roger McGough for a poem from *Gig* (Jonathan Cape);

Eric Millward for a poem from *Dead Letters* (Harry Chambers/ Peterloo Poets);

Adrian Mitchell for three poems from *Out Loud* and *Ride The Nightmare* (Cape Goliard Press);

The Estate of Ogden Nash for a poem from *I'm A Stranger Here Myself* (Gollancz, 1938);

Mrs Sonia Brownell Orwell for George Orwell's dedication to *Keep The Aspidistra Flying* (Martin Secker & Warburg);

Gerald Duckworth & Co Ltd for a poem from *The Best Of Dorothy Parker*;

Tom Pickard for a poem from *High On The Walls* (Fulcrum, 1967);

The Estate of William Plomer and Sir Rupert Hart-Davis for five poems from *Collected Poems* (Cape);

Faber & Faber Ltd and New Directions Publishing Corp. for an extract from *The Cantos Of Ezra Pound*;

Graham Chapman, John Cleese, Terry Gilliam, Eric Idle, Terry Jones and Michael Palin for verses from *Monty Python's Life Of Brian* (Eyre Methuen) © 1979 Python Productions Ltd;

Olga Katzin (Sagittarius) for three poems, two of them first published in the *New Statesman* and one previously unpublished;

Mr G. T. Sassoon for three poems by Siegfried Sassoon;

Rosalind Wade for a poem from *Collected Poems* by William Kean Seymour (Robert Hale, 1946);

C. H. Sisson for four poems, two of which are from *In The Trojan Ditch* (Carcanet), one from *The London Zoo* (Abelard Schuman) and one previously unpublished;

Osbert Sitwell for a poem from *The Winstonburg Line: Three Satires* (Henderson's, 1919);

James MacGibbon, the Executor of the Estate of Stevie Smith, for four poems from *The Collected Poems Of Stevie Smith* (Allen Lane);

Jon Stallworthy for a poem from *Root And Branch* (Chatto & Windus);

Professor J. P. Sullivan for a poem from *The Jaundiced Eye, Poems & Satires* (Buffalo, New York, 1976);

Mr Hubert Nicholson, Literary Executor of the Estate of A. S. J. Tessimond, for a poem from *Not Love Perhaps . . .* (Autolycus Press);

Judith Viorst and the New American Library for a poem from *It's Hard To Be Hip Over Thirty And Other Tragedies Of Married*

Life by Judith Viorst. Reprinted by arrangement with the New American Library, Inc., New York, New York;

Faber & Faber Ltd and Harcourt Brace Jovanovich, Inc. for a poem by Richard Wilbur from *Poems 1943-1956*;

Roger Woddis for a poem from *The Woddis Collection* (Hutchinsons) and two poems first published in the *New Statesman*;

Miss Ann Wolfe for a poem by Humbert Wolfe from *The Uncelestial City* (Gollancz, 1930);

Michael and Ann Yeats and Macmillan London Ltd for three poems by W. B. Yeats from *Collected Poems*.

Every effort has been made to trace copyright holders, but in some cases they could not be found. The editor and publishers wish to apologise for consequent omissions.

The editor wishes also to thank Geoffrey Strachan of Eyre Methuen for his enthusiasm and advice in the fashioning of this work.

Textual Note: Where the original text of a poem has been abridged, omissions from the original are indicated by three dots following the full stop. Where a title has been given to an extract from a long poem the original title of the poem is given after the poet's name.

INTRODUCTION

Why, you may ask, should there be an anthology of the poetry of hatred and abuse? My first answer is that hate is as powerful an emotion as love. It is not so frequently expressed but it can be as intense. It is a negative and destructive emotion, and moral teaching throughout the centuries has been directed to discouraging its manifestation and to stifling its effect. However, hatred and scorn of the stupid, the vain, the vicious, the venal and the cruel promote feelings of hostility to those things which can change them for the better. This was Auden's defence of such poetry:

Satire is angry and optimistic – it believes that once people's attention is drawn to some evil, they will mend their ways.

Secondly, English poetry is particularly rich in satire and invective. Some of the most quoted phrases which are now used in ordinary speech, such as Pope's 'to damn with faint praise', come from satirical attacks. Much of this poetry is witty and some of it very funny. It is also very enjoyable to read, for there is in most people a lurking tendency to laugh at the misfortunes of others particularly when they are pompous and absurd. In *Don Juan* Byron noted the delight that the true hater experiences:

Hatred is by far the longest pleasure
Men love in haste but they detest at leisure.

Satirical poetry has therefore an aim – to ridicule something or someone that has offended the poet. It is not merely vulgar abuse. There is some poetry that is just that, but it soon palls as the pejorative adjectives and invective exhaust themselves through repetition.

Satirical poetry is more subtle and disciplined. Its weapons are more finely wrought than the bludgeon of invective. Dryden, the father of English satirical poetry, laid down rules very clearly;

19

The nicest and most delicate touches of satire consist of fine raillery . . . how easy it is to call rogue and villain and that wittily! But how hard to make a man appear a fool, a blockhead and knave without using any of those opprobrious terms! . . . There is still a vast difference betwixt the slovenly butchering of a man, and the fineness of a stroke that separates the head from the body, and leaves it standing in its place.

The finest poems in this collection do just that. Dryden's famous description of the Duke of Buckingham, 'Stiff in opinions, always in the wrong; was everything by starts and nothing long'; William Plomer's description of a rich homosexual, 'A rose-red cissy half as old as time'; Max Beerbohm's cool disdain for George V and Queen Mary; Chesterton's question to the humbug politician, 'Are they clinging to their crosses, F. E. Smith?' and Adrian Mitchell's 'Tell me lies about Vietnam'. These are all acts of poetical assassination which achieve their object through cleverness and subtlety.

Satire is also public poetry, for its objects are people in the public eye, kings, politicians, churchmen, lawyers, bankers or other poets; or activities that the writers don't like, such as modern property development, cruelty to animals or evident injustice. The purpose of the poet is to create a strong feeling which may harden into a conviction, and which may in its turn be sharpened into action. Action to put right the wrong can only occur if the poet passes the message to a wider audience. Political verse is therefore essentially propaganda. The best poems in this anthology are the most ferocious since they evoke anger or contempt or pity.

Certain events have also inspired hatred and scorn, the most striking example being the First World War. The horror of the fighting in the trenches for four years; the death of hundreds of thousands of men; and the sheer futility of the whole exercise produced a great outburst of poetry, which is some of the most remarkable of the century. There are many anthologies of war poetry where you will find the now famous attacks by Sassoon and Owen. I have included some of the lesser known poems and a particularly bitter one written by Kipling after the death of his son John at the battle of Loos. This sort of poetry did not start in 1914 and end in 1918. There have been misgivings down the ages from Robert Burns to e. e. cummings on the Russian invasion of Hungary and to Padraic Fiacc on Ulster. The suffering of Northern Ireland has produced some very fine poetry from both sides of the border.

The Second World War produced duller poetry than the First. There was no poet for our finest hour – the prose of Churchill caught the spirit of Britain. The real horrors of that war occurred in the concentration camps, and they were too horrific for either prose or poetry. The newsreels of Belsen and Dachau were the devastating memorials to Nazi cruelty. There is surprisingly little poetry against Hitler and Nazism even in the 1930s. One of the most sustained attacks on Nazism is the long poem by Hugh MacDiarmid, 'The Battle Continues', which was written in the thirties but not published until 1957. Sagittarius wrote a weekly parody for the *New Statesman*, and I have included her description of Hitler and Mussolini meeting on a railway station which brings back to the inward eye the funniest scene in Chaplin's *Great Dictator*.

So you will not find in this anthology many intimate personal poems about a poet's inner feelings. The poetry is about public things, and usually important and big things. The bigger the target the better the verse, for as Milton said:

For a satire as it was born out of tragedy so ought to ressemble his parentage to strike high and adventure dangerously at the most emminent vices among the greatest persons, and not to creep into every blind taphouse that fears a constable more than a satire.

The largest section of this anthology is, not surprisingly, about politicians. My chosen profession has been the greatest butt of satire. The sharpest attacks started on the return of Charles II in 1660. The freedom and licence of that age has frequently been criticised and compared unfavourably to the seemly decorum of the Commonwealth. One of the fruits of that freedom was a flood of frank and libellous poetry on the King by Rochester, and on politicians by Dryden. This was the start of the great period of English satiric verse.

Dryden was followed by Pope and Swift, and the three together created the high water mark of English satire. Swift

21

was the most bitter, particularly in his descriptions of women. I have included an extract from one of these poems, though I have little doubt that if it appeared today for the first time, it would be roundly condemned. He felt neglected in his exile in Ireland and his swelling indignation, growing more intense and vicious, drove him finally to madness. When Addison and Steel founded *The Spectator* they established the sentimental approach, and their kindliness seeped through and withered the roots of satire. It revived a bit at the end of the eighteenth century, principally because George III and George IV provided such good targets. But the best satire was visual, in Gillray's cartoons. Some of Byron's poetry was angry, but not with the intensity found at the beginning of the century.

Then the pall of Victorian respectability descended. Sentimentality and what was deemed proper for the parlour wounded satire, and *Punch* dealt the final blow. It was not until the end of Victoria's reign that a few cheeky people poked their noses out of the blanket and started their irreverent attacks on individuals and institutions: Shaw, Beerbohm, Belloc, Chesterton, Kipling and Lawrence.

Not all satiric poets want to reform. Some just want to describe a particular person or profession or a social custom that they don't like. For some the line between love and hatred is finely drawn. In his poem, 'County', Betjeman scornfully lashes the English County families, but deep down one feels that he really rather likes them. The same is true of Noel Coward's lyric, 'Children of the Ritz'. This is particularly true of xenophobic poetry. But you will find that the strongest attacks on England come from English poets, weeping at her sick bed.

The social targets of satire don't seem to have changed very much over the centuries. The anonymous attack on marriage in the sixteenth century is echoed rather more gently by the contemporary American poet Judith Viorst. D. H. Lawrence's comments on elderly discontented women recall Dryden's translation of Juvenal's bitter description of old age, and Johnson on gold finds an heir in Louis MacNeice on property. Another constant strand in satirical poetry is a contempt for worldly success. Pope in the eighteenth century and Betjeman in the twentieth century in their sharp attacks on the pushy and nouveaux riches also express a preference for the older, traditional and more responsible virtues of a rural society. Their heroes are those who put public good before personal profit.

One of the striking things about satirical poetry is that the poets of the Right, the defenders of ancient virtues, have been more successful than the poets of the Left. The Left are all too eager to grab the nearest bludgeon and to start on the 'slovenly butchering of a man'. The poets of the Left are also at a disadvantage in that few of them have any humour. The nature of humour is conservative, which is why over the centuries good Left-wing wits and humorists are few and far between.

One thing that unites the poets of the Right and the Left is their contempt for anyone who attempts to patronise them. Johnson in the eighteenth century and Wyndham Lewis in the twentieth century both felt keenly the humiliation of being obliged to people whom they not unreasonably regarded as inferior. Christopher Logue expressed the same sentiment in the introduction to the little book of songs that he wrote for the 'Establishment' Night Club in Soho.

> Morals pay well – I must confess.
> Farting through silk helps me express
> Satire's principle: Unless
> You bite the hand from which you've fed
> It will pat you on the head.

Satire and caricature found their post-war feet again in Britain in the early 1960s when thirteen years of Tory government provided a good target, and there was also the feeling that all the old standards and rules that had served Britain well in the past had perversely turned upon her, and helped to drag her down. The magazine *Private Eye*, the 'Establishment' and the television programme 'That Was The Week That Was' all epitomise this period. Christopher Logue and Adrian Mitchell wrote angry poems but then the muse of satire dozed for a bit. She has stirred again now. Roger Woddis contributes brilliant parodies to the *New Statesman* and C. H. Sisson can explode with a stringent outburst. I have been able to include several poems written in the last few years by Elizabeth Bartlett, Edward Bond and Anthony Hecht which

23

are powerful satirical attacks upon the old enemies which Pope and Dryden battled against.

I do appreciate the difficulties that beset a satirical poet today. Satirical verse needs as its ground a strong and confident literary tradition. It requires scholarship and a disciplined restraint. The target must be caught, pinned down and preserved like a butterfly in a case. It also requires an audience that appreciates wit and style, and which is reflective and thoughtful.

Satire also needs heroes, as well as the pathetic pretenders to the heroic. This is not an heroic age and even the pretenders are half-hearted. So the targets are shadowy. The flamboyant and the absurd still abound but they conduct their buffooneries in financial frauds and frivolous jet-setting. They are not important enough for the venomed dart, merely the pinprick of the gossip column.

Yet there is still great injustice, hypocrisy and poverty in the world. Where are today's satirical poets to describe for example the simple purity of Islamic justice? Or the uncorrupt government that lightens the lot of most Africans? Or the great advance of psychotherapy that is being 'pioneered' in Soviet 'hospitals'? Or the conspicuous consumption of the West that is needed to generate the funds for the starving poor of India?

These are all prime targets, and poets with a satiric vein should follow Milton's advice, 'to strike high and adventure dangerously'. To hit these targets the poet has the most effective weapon, his own words and his ability to put them together in a memorable and striking way. In an age of wanton violence the lethal accuracy of the poet is as much to be valued as ever. As Auden said,

I have no gun but I can spit.

KENNETH BAKER

24

I Have No Gun But I Can Spit

Some thirty inches from my nose
The frontier of my Person goes,
And all the untilled air between
Is private *pagus* or demesne.
Stranger, unless with bedroom cyes
I beckon you to fraternize,
Beware of rudely crossing it:
I have no gun, but I can spit.

W. H. AUDEN
from *The Birth Of Architecture*

Men Worship Venus Everywhere

Extempore Pinned To A Lady's Coach

If you rattle along like your mistress's tongue,
  Your speed will outrival the dart;
But a fly for your load, you'll break down on the road,
  If your stuff be as rotten's her heart.

ROBERT BURNS

Pangloss's Song*

Dear boy, you will not hear me speak
  With sorrow or with rancour
Of what has paled my rosy cheek
  And blasted it with canker;
'Twas Love, great Love, that did the deed
  Through Nature's gentle laws,
And how should ill effects proceed
  From so divine a cause?

Sweet honey comes from bees that sting,
  As you are well aware;
To one adept in reasoning,
  Whatever pains disease may bring
Are but the tangy seasoning
  To Love's delicious fare.

Columbus and his men, they say,
  Conveyed the virus hither
Whereby my features rot away
  And vital powers wither;
Yet had they not traversed the seas
  And come infected back,
Why, think of all the luxuries
  That modern life would lack!

*The American poet, Richard Wilbur, wrote the lyrics for a musical version
of Voltaire's *Candide* in 1956. Dr Pangloss is the incurable optimist, who, in
spite of being let down time and time again, continues to believe that 'all is
for the best in the best of all possible worlds.'

31

All bitter things conduce to sweet,
    As this example shows;
Without the little spirochete
    We'd have no chocolate to eat,
Nor would tobacco's fragrance greet
    The European nose.

Each nation guards its native land
    With cannon and with sentry,
Inspectors look for contraband
    At every port of entry,
Yet nothing can prevent the spread
    Of Love's divine disease;
It rounds the world from bed to bed
    As pretty as you please.

Men worship Venus everywhere,
    As plainly may be seen;
The decorations which I bear
    Are nobler than the Croix de Guerre,
And gained in service of our fair
And universal Queen.

                              RICHARD WILBUR

Directed To That
Inconsiderable Animal Called Husband

Husband! thou dull unpittied miscreant,
Wedded to noise, to misery, and want;
Sold an eternal vassall for thy life,
Oblig'd to cherish and to heat a wife:
Repeat thy loath'd embraces every night
Prompted to act, by duty not delight.
Christen thy froward bantling every Year,
And carefully thy spurious issue rear.
Go once a week to see the brat at nurse,
And let the young impostor drain thy purse:
·Marry'd! O Hell and Furies! Name it not,
Hence, hence you holy cheats; a plot, a plot!

32

By day 'tis nothing but an endless noise;
By night the eccho of forgotten joys:
Ye gods! that man by his own slavish Law,
Should on himself such inconvenience draw.
Pox on him! let him go: what can I say?
Anathemas on him are thrown away;
The wretch is marry'd, and has known the worst,
And now his blessing is, he can't be curst.

ANON 1690

Vagabond Love

They made love under bridges, lacking beds,
And engines whistled them a bridal song,
A sudden bull's-eye showed them touching heads,
Policemen told them they were doing wrong;

And when they slept on seats in public gardens
Told them, 'Commit no nuisance in the park';
The beggars, begging the policemen's pardons,
Said that they thought as it was after dark –

At this the law grew angry and declared
Outlaws who outrage by-laws are the devil;
At this, the lovers only stood and stared,
As well they might, for they had meant no evil;
'Move on,' the law said. To avoid a scene
They moved. And thus we keep our cities clean.

WILLIAM PLOMER

An Old Malediction

What well-heeled knuckle-head, straight from the unisex
Hairstylist and bathed in *Russian Leather*,
Dallies with you these late summer days, Pyrrha,
In your expensive sublet? For whom do you
Slip into something simple by, say, Gucci?

33

The more fool he who has mapped out for himself
The saline latitudes of incontinent grief.
Dazzled though he be, poor dope, by the golden looks
Your locks fetched up out of a bottle of *Clairol*,
He will know that the wind changes, the smooth sailing
Is done for, when the breakers wallop him broadside,
When he's rudderless, dismasted, thoroughly swamped
In that mindless rip-tide that got the best of me
Once, when I ventured on your deeps, Piranha.

ANTHONY HECHT
freely adapted from Horace

A Moolie Besom

Wi' every effort to be fair
And nae undue antagonism
I canna but say that my sweethert's mither
Is a moolie besom, a moolie besom,
    Naething but a moolie besom!

Am I no' feart Jean'll turn the same?
Her mither was aince as bonny as her.
Sae what's mair likely she'll become in turn
Her vieve een dull, face lourd that's noo kir,
    Naething but a moolie besom?

HUGH MacDIARMID

Sweet Celia's Boudoir

. . . Five hours, (and who can do it less in?)
By haughty Celia spent in dressing;
The goddess from her chamber issues,
Array'd in lace, brocades, and tissues.
Strephon, who found the room was void,
And Betty otherwise employ'd,

Stole in, and took a strict Survey
Of all the litter as it lay:
Whereof, to make the matter clear,
An inventory follows here.

And first a dirty smock appeared,
Beneath the arm-pits well besmeared,
Strephon, the rogue, display'd it wide,
And turn'd it round on ev'ry side:
In such a case few words are best,
And Strephon bids us guess the rest:
But swears, how damnably the men lie
In calling Celia sweet and cleanly.

Now listen, while he next produces
The various combs for various uses,
Fill'd up with dirt so closely fixt,
No brush cou'd force a way betwixt;
A paste of composition rare,
Sweat, dandruff, powder, lead and hair.
A forehead-cloth with oil upon't
To smooth the wrinkles on her front:

Some fill'd with washes, some with paste;
Some with pomatums, paints, and slops,
And ointments good for scabby chops.
Hard by a filthy bason stands,
Foul'd with the scowring of her hands;
The bason takes whatever comes,
The scrapings from her teeth and gums,
A nasty compound of all hues,
For here she spits, and here she spues.

But oh! it turn'd poor Strephon's bowels,
When he beheld and smelt the towels,
Begumm'd, bematter'd, and beslim'd,
With dirt, and sweat, and ear-wax grim'd,
No object Strephon's eye escapes,
Here petticoats in frowzy heaps;
Nor be the handkerchiefs forgot,
All varnish'd o'er with snuff and snot.

The stockings why should I expose,
Stain'd with the moisture of her toes,
Or greasy coifs, or pinners reeking,
Which Celia slept at least a week in.
A pair of tweezers next he found,
To pluck her brows in arches round,
Or hairs that sink the forehead low,
Or on her chin like bristles grow . . .

JONATHAN SWIFT
from *The Lady's Dressing Room*

Remember Thee!*

Remember thee! Remember thee!
   Till Lethe quench life's burning streams
Remorse and shame shall cling to thee
   And haunt thee like a feverish dream
Remember thee! Ay, doubt it not,
   Thy husband too shall think of thee,
By neither shalt thou be forgot,
   Thou false to him, thou fiend to me!

LORD BYRON

*In 1812 Caroline Lamb, the young and beautiful wife of the politician, William Lamb, who was to become known as Melbourne, fell in love with Byron. After their first meeting she noted in her journal that he was 'Mad, bad, and dangerous to know'. The affair was played out in the full glare of London society. Byron soon pulled out of her hysterical possessiveness and at a Ball in 1813 she tried to commit suicide by slashing her wrists.

She invaded Byron's rooms and finding a copy of Beckford's *Vathek* lying open, scrawled 'Remember me' across the title page. Byron followed her advice in this bitter little poem.

Girls' Chorus

Just let a man into your house
And he will ask for bread;
Just spread the table in your house
And he will seek your bed;
A moment on your bed and he
Will make himself your Mister,
Then rested, comfy, and well fed,
He'll seduce your sister.

CHRISTOPHER LOGUE

On First Looking Through Krafft-Ebing's Psychopathia Sexualis*

Much have I travelled in those realms of old
Where many a whore in hall-doors could be seen
Of many a bonnie brothel or shebeen
Which bawds connived at by policemen hold.
I too have listened when the Quay was coaled,
But never did I taste the Pure Obscene —
Much less imagine that my past was clean —
Till this Krafft-Ebing out his story told.
Then felt I rather taken by surprise
As on the evening when I met Macran,
And retrospective thoughts and doubts did rise —
Was I quite normal when my life began
With love that leans towards rural sympathies
Potent behind a cart with Mary Ann?

OLIVER ST JOHN GOGARTY

*Krafft-Ebing was the German professor of psychiatry who in the late nineteenth century pioneered the study of criminal psychology and sexual deviation. H. S. Macran was a philosopher, of Trinity College, Dublin.

37

The Playboy Of The Demi-World

Aloft in Heavenly Mansions, Doubleyou One –
Just Mayfair flats, but certainly sublime –
You'll find the abode of D'Arcy Honeybunn,
A rose-red sissy half as old as time.

Peace cannot age him, and no war could kill
The genial tenant of those cosy rooms,
He's lived there always and he lives there still,
Perennial pansy, hardiest of blooms.

There you'll encounter aunts of either sex,
Their jokes equivocal or over-ripe,
Ambiguous couples wearing slacks and specs
And the stout Lesbian knocking out her pipe.

The rooms are crammed with flowers and objets d'art,
A Ganymede still hands the drinks – and plenty!
D'Arcy still keeps a rakish-looking car
And still behaves the way he did at twenty.

A ruby pin is fastened in his tie,
The scent he uses is *Adieu Sagesse,*
His shoes are suède, and as the years go by
His tailor's bill's not getting any less.

He cannot whistle, always rises late,
Is good at indoor sports and parlour tricks,
Mauve is his favourite colour, and his gait
Suggests a peahen walking on hot bricks.

He prances forward with his hands outspread
And folds all comers in a gay embrace,
A wavy toupee on his hairless head,
A fixed smile on his often-lifted face.

My dear!' he lisps, to whom all men are dear,
'How perfectly enchanting of you!'; turns
Towards his guests and twitters, 'Look who's here!
Do come and help us fiddle while Rome burns!'

'The kindest man alive,' so people say,
'Perpetual youth!' But have you seen his eyes?
The eyes of some old saurian in decay,
That asks no questions and is told no lies.

Under the fribble lurks a worn-out sage
Heavy with disillusion, and alone;
So never say to D'Arcy, 'Be your age!' –
He'd shrivel up at once or turn to stone.

WILLIAM PLOMER

Correction

Delete 'Wax Effigy, some Pins, one Witch'.
Insert 'One Lawyer, one Vindictive Bitch'.

ERIC MILLWARD

Bronxville Darby And Joan

We do not fear the verdict of posterity,
Our lives have been too humdrum and mundane,
In the twilight of our days
Having reached the final phase
In all sincerity
We must explain:

We're a dear old couple and we HATE one another
And we've hated one another for a long, long time.
Since the day that we were wed, up to the present,
Our lives, we must confess,
Have been progressively more unpleasant.

39

We're just sweet old darlings who despise one another
With a thoroughness approaching the sublime,
But through all our years
We've been affectionately known
As the Bronxville Darby and Joan.

Our Golden Wedding passed with all our family,
An orgy of remembrance and rue,
In acknowledgement of this
We exchanged a loving kiss
A trifle clammily
Because we knew:

We're a dear old couple who DETEST one another,
We've detested one another since our bridal night,
Which was squalid, unattractive and convulsive
And proved, beyond dispute,
That we were mutually repulsive.
We're just sweet old darlings who torment one another
With the utmost maliciousness and spite,
And through all our years
We've been inaccurately known
As the Bronxville Darby and Joan.

We're a dear old couple and we LOATHE one another
With a loathing that engulfs us like a tidal wave,
With our deep sub-conscious minds we seldom dabble
But something *must* impel
The words we spell
When we're playing 'Scrabble'.
We're just sweet old darlings who abhor one another
And we'll bore each other firmly to the grave,
But through all our years we've been referred to
    more or less
As the Bronxville Porgy and Bess.

NOEL COWARD
from Sail Away

Where Is It Written?

Where is it written
That husbands get twenty-five-dollar lunches and invitations
    to South America for think conferences while
Wives get Campbell's black bean soup and a trip to the
    firehouse with the first grade and
Where is it written
That husbands get to meet beautiful lady lawyers and
    beautiful lady professors of Ancient History and beautiful
    sculptresses and heiresses and poetesses while
Wives get to meet the checker with the acne at the Safeway
    and
Where is it written
That husbands get a nap and the Super Bowl on Sundays
    while
Wives get to help color in the coloring book and
Where is it written
That husbands get ego gratification, emotional support, and
    hot tea in bed for ten days when they have the sniffles
    while
Wives get to give it to them?

And if a wife should finally decide
Let him take the shoes to the shoemaker and the children to
    the pediatrician and the dog to the vet while she takes up
    something like brain surgery or transcendental meditation,
Where is it written
That she always has to feel
Guilty?

                                                    JUDITH VIORST

Money The She-Devil

Money

I was led into captivity by the bitch business
Not in love but in what seemed a physical necessity
And now I cannot even watch the spring
The itch for subsistence having become responsibility.

Money the she-devil comes to us under many veils
Tactful at first, calling herself beauty
Tear away this disguise, she proposes paternal solicitude
Assuming the dishonest face of duty.

Suddenly you are in bed with a screeching tear-sheet
This is money at last without her night-dress
Clutching you against her fallen udders and sharp bones
In an unscrupulous and deserved embrace.

C. H. SISSON

On Gold

But scarce observ'd, the knowing and the bold
Fall in the gen'ral massacre of gold;
Wide-wasting pest! that rages unconfin'd,
And crowds with crimes the records of mankind;

For gold his sword the hireling ruffian draws,
For gold the hireling judge distorts the laws;
Wealth heap'd on wealth, nor truth nor safety buys,
The dangers gather as the treasures rise.

SAMUEL JOHNSON
from The Vanity of Human Wishes

On Property

Property! Property! Let us extend
Soul and body without end:
A box to live in, with airs and graces,
A box on wheels that shows its paces,
A box that talks or that makes faces,
And curtains and fences as good as the neighbours'
To keep out the neighbours and keep us immured
Enjoying the cold canned fruit of our labours
In a sterilised cell, unshared, insured.

Property! Property! When will it end?
When will the Poltergeist ascend
Out of the sewer with chopper and squib
To burn the mink and the baby's bib
And cut the tattling wire to town
And smash all the plastics, clowning and clouting,
And stop all the boxes shouting and pouting
And wreck the house from the aerial down
And give these ingrown souls an outing?

LOUIS MacNEICE
from *Jigsaws*

On Bankers

A baited banker thus desponds,
From his own hand foresees his fall,
They have his soul who have his bonds,
'Tis like the writing on the wall.

How will the caitiff wretch be scar'd
When first he finds himself awake
At the last trumpet, unprepar'd,
And all his grand account to make?

46

For in that universall call
Few bankers will to heav'n be mounters:
They'll cry, ye shops, upon us fall
Conceal, and cover us, ye counters.

When other hands the scales shall hold,
And they in men and angels sight
Produc'd with all their bills and gold,
Weigh'd in the ballance, and found light.

JONATHAN SWIFT
from *The Run Upon the Bankers*

Bankers Are Just Like Anybody Else, Except Richer

This is a song to celebrate banks,
Because they are full of money and you go into them and all
    you hear is clinks and clanks,
Or maybe a sound like the wind in the trees on the hills,
Which is the rustling of the thousand dollar bills.
Most bankers dwell in marble halls,
Which they get to dwell in because they encourage deposits
    and discourage withdralls,
And particularly because they all observe one rule which woe
    betides the banker who fails to heed it,
Which is you must never lend any money to anybody unless
    they don't need it.
I know you, you cautious conservative banks!
If people are worried about their rent it is your duty to deny
    them the loan of one nickel, yes, even one copper
    engraving of the martyred son of the late Nancy Hanks;
Yes, if they request fifty dollars to pay for a baby you must
    look at them like Tarzan looking at an uppity ape in the
    jungle,
And tell them what do they think a bank is, anyhow, they
    had better go get the money from their wife's aunt or
    ungle.

But suppose people come in and they have a million and they
    want another million to pile on top of it,
Why, you brim with the milk of human kindness and you
    urge them to accept every drop of it,
And you lend them the million so then they have two million
    and this gives them the idea that they would be better off
    with four.
So they already have two million as security so you have no
    hesitation in lending them two more,
And all the vice-presidents nod their heads in rhythm,
And the only question asked is do the borrowers want the
    money sent or do they want to take it withm.
But please do not think that I am not fond of banks,
Because I think they deserve our appreciation and thanks,
Because they perform a valuable public service in eliminating
    the jackasses who go around saying that health and
    happiness are everything and money isn't essential,
Because as soon as they have to borrow some unimportant
    money to maintain their health and happiness they starve
    to death so they can't go around any more sneering at
    good old money, which is nothing short of providential.

OGDEN NASH

The Poor Man And The Rich
(On The Sabbath)

The poor man's sins are glaring;
In the face of ghostly warning
    He is caught in the fact
    Of an overt act –
Buying greens on a Sunday morning.

The rich man's sins are hidden,
In the pomp of wealth and station;
    And escape the sight
    Of the children of light,
Who are wise in their generation.

48

The rich man has a kitchen,
And cooks to dress his dinner;
　　The poor who would roast
　　To the baker's must post,
And thus become a sinner.

The rich man has a cellar,
And a ready butler by him;
　　The poor must steer
　　For his pint of beer
Where the saint can't choose but spy him.

The rich man's painted windows
Hide the concerts of the quality;
　　The poor can but share
　　A crack'd fiddle in the air,
Which offends all sound morality.

The rich man is invisible
In the crowd of his gay society;
　　But the poor man's delight
　　Is a sore in the sight,
And a stench in the nose of piety.

The rich man has a carriage
Where no rude eye can flout him;
　　The poor man's bane
　　Is a third-class train,
With the daylight all about him.

The rich man goes out yachting,
Where sanctity can't pursue him;
　　The poor goes afloat
　　In a fourpenny boat,
Where the bishop groans to view him.

T. L. PEACOCK

The Decadent Voyeurs

They pass factories and pits and poverty
in flashy cars, and spit;
and return to coal warm fires
which from the earth
these other men have ripped.

TOM PICKARD

On Money*

Though I speak with the tongues of men and of angels, and
have not money, I am become as a sounding brass, or a tinkling
cymbal. And though I have the gift of prophecy, and under-
stand all mysteries, and all knowledge; and though I have all
faith, so that I could remove mountains, and have not money, I
am nothing. And though I bestow all my goods to feed the
poor, and though I give my body to be burned, and have not
money, it profiteth me nothing. Money suffereth long, and is
kind; money envieth not; money vaunteth not itself, is not
puffed up, doth not behave unseemly, seeketh not her own, is
not easily provoked, thinketh no evil; rejoiceth not in iniquity,
but rejoiceth in the truth; beareth all things, believeth all
things, hopeth all things, endureth all things . . . And now
abideth faith, hope, money, these three; but the greatest of
these is money.

ST PAUL AND GEORGE ORWELL
from *The Authorized Version,*
1 Corinthians, Chapter 13 (adapted)

*This was the dedication by George Orwell to his novel *Keep the Aspidistra
Flying*. He transposed only one word in this famous passage from St Paul on
Faith, Hope and Charity, but this one change sums up Orwell's contempt for
all wordly goods.

50

The British Workman And The Government

Hold my hand, Auntie, Auntie,
Auntie, hold my hand!
I feel I'm going to be naughty, Auntie,
and you don't seem to understand.

Hold my hand and love me, Auntie,
love your little boy!
We want to be loved, especially, Auntie,
us whom you can't employ.

Idle we stand by the kerb–edge, Auntie,
dangling our useless hands.
But we don't mind so much if you love us, and we feel
that Auntie understands.

                          D. H. LAWRENCE

*England Of Cant
And Smug Discretion*

The Well-Extracted Blood Of Englishmen

Thus from a mixture of all kinds began
That heterogeneous thing, an Englishman:
In eager rapes and furious lusts begot
Betwixt a painted Briton and a Scot:
Whose gend'ring offspring quickly learn'd to bow
And yoke their heifers to the Roman plow;
From whence a mongrel, half-bred race there came,
With neither name nor nation, speech or fame,
In whose hot veins new mixtures quickly ran,
Infus'd betwixt a Saxon and a Dane;
While their rank daughters, to their parents just,
Receiv'd all nations with promiscuous lust.
This nauseous brood directly did contain
The well-extracted blood of Englishmen.

DANIEL DEFOE
from *The True-born Englishman*

General Bloodstock's Lament For England

[This image (seemingly animated) walks with them in the fields
in broad Day-light; and if they are employed in delving, harrow-
ing, Seed-sowing or any other Occupation, they are at the same
time mimicked by the ghostly Visitant. Men of the Second Sight
... call this reflex-man a Co-walker, every way like the Man, as
his Twin-brother and Companion, haunting as his Shadow.

Kirk's *Secret Commonwealth,* 1691.]

Alas, England, my own generous mother,
One gift I have from you I hate,
The second sight: I see your weird co-walker,
Silver-zoned Albion, stepping in your track,
Mimicking your sad and doubtful gait,
Your clasped hands, your head-shakings, your bent back.

The white hem of a winding sheet
Draws slowly upward from her feet;
Soon it will mount knee-high, then to the thigh.
It crackles like the parchment of the treaties,
Bonds, contracts and conveyances,
With which, beggared and faint and like to die,
You signed away your island sovereignty
To rogues who learned their primer at your knees.

ROBERT GRAVES

Drink, Britannia

Drink, Britannia, Britannia, drink your Tea,
For Britons, Boars and butter'd Toast; they all begin with B.

THOMAS LOVELL BEDDOES

England

Autumn 1938

Plush bees above a bed of dahlias;
    Leisurely, timeless garden teas;
Brown bread and honey; scent of mowing;
    The still green light below tall trees.

The ancient custom of deception;
    A Press that seldom stoops to lies –
Merely suppresses truth and twists it,
    Blandly corrupt and slyly wise.

The Common Man; his mask of laughter;
    His back-chat while the roof falls in;
Minorities' long losing battles
    Fought that the sons of sons may win.

56

The politician's inward snigger
  (Big business on the private phone);
The knack of sitting snug on fences;
  The double face of flesh and stone.

Grape-bloom of distant woods at dusk;
  Storm-crown on Glaramara's head;
The fire-rose over London night;
  An old plough rusting autumn-red.

The 'incorruptible policeman'
  Gaoling the whore whose bribe's run out,
Guarding the rich against the poor man,
  Guarding the Settled Gods from doubt.

The generous smile of music-halls,
  Bars and bank-holidays and queues;
The private peace of public foes;
  The truce of pipe and football news.

The smile of privilege exultant;
  Smile at the 'bloody Red' defeated;
Smile at the striker starved and broken;
  Smile at the 'dirty nigger' cheated.

The old hereditary craftsman;
  The incommunicable skill;
The pride in long-loved tools, refusal
  To do the set job quick or ill.

The greater artist mocked, misflattered;
  The lesser forming clique and team,
Or crouching in his narrow corner,
  Narcissus with his secret dream.

England of rebels – Blake and Shelley;
  England where freedom's sometimes won,
Where Jew and Negro needn't fear yet
  Lynch-law and pogrom, whip and gun.

England of cant and smug discretion;
    England of wagecut-sweatshop-knight,
Of sportsman-churchman-slum-exploiter,
Of puritan grown sour with spite.

England of clever fool, mad genius,
    Timorous lion and arrogant sheep,
Half-hearted snob and shamefaced bully,
    Of hands that wake and eyes that sleep...
England the snail that's shod with lightning...
    Shall we laugh or shall we weep?

                                A. S. J. TESSIMOND

The English

Many of the English,
The intelligent English,
Of the Arts, the Professions and the Upper Middle Classes,
Are under-cover men,
But what is under the cover
(That was original)
Died; now they are corpse-carriers.
It is not noticeable, but be careful,
They are infective.

                                STEVIE SMITH

The North*

Living in the North one gets used to the cold nights
The cities, like stone tongues in the valleys
And the lugged crowds, daft zombies, poured through the
    streets.

The cities are strewn across the North
Like mucky snags that grace a miner's back. . . .

*Brian Higgins produced only three volumes of poetry before he died in
1965. He was born in Yorkshire in 1930. No poet has quite captured the
flavour of the North of England as he did in this poem.

58

Liverpool, huge and lewd, roaring with black men and knives
And orange angers of race quarrels
Which have never been much more than a chaos of violent
    bad temper.
Race, the formality of an excuse.
If you do it for love or money and you're under twenty
They call you a teddy boy.
Manchester, bigger still, the great pale face of Lancashire.
Spewn in useless fly-blown shops and prosperous slums;
A ganglion of rotting and roaring industrialism
A monstrous rancour of wheels and payment
From glass blowing St. Helens to the grease-filled
    passageways of Oldham. . . .

Then Huddersfield, Halifax, Bradford and Leeds
With a few banal remarks about the juxtaposition of muck
    and money;
The two Great Novelists of Bradford, Braine and Priestley
Who sell their novels like so many bales of wool
– Most of them about Batley
Where the rag merchants marry chorus girls
But not, one supposes, for breeding purposes
To salt the pedigree and let a bit of red blood into the strain.
There isn't much that's selective in a rag-merchant's
    ancestry. . . .

The stark rectangle of Hull
With its bombed squares filling up even now
Twenty years after the luftwaffe gave it a going over
Stands by the wide desolation of the Humber.
A cold clean city full of new pubs.
With the worst University in England
Peopled with foreman-lecturers jostling to get reviews in the
    Guardian
Even their names sound like pieces of machinery. . . .

The new proletarian intellectuals
Who have beer and darts parties ('My father was a crane
    driver')
All the uniform muddle of the New Left

Competing like hell to get their articles published.
And Lucky-Jimming it up to senior lecturer.
Pretending to boast about having a refrigerator
But really winking at knowing what refrigerators stand for.
Interviewing the surrounding chaos and Insurance Stamping
     us to Elysium
Till their cellars burst and the statistics rattle the ceiling
(I'd rather jump into a tank full of Chablis and to hell with the
     social survey
And social justice into the bargain, if that's what they call it)
DON'T BLAME ME: I'M NOT ADAM. . . .

I am the boreal singer. I am North.
I know and hate the factories that made me
The nouveau riche wool magnates with their daughters
Brass bound for Roedean, and their sons
'One's i't business, t'other lad's at Oxford.'
The two-gun culture of the busy rich
Who live in Ilkley and who work in Batley
Dealing in grease, wool bales and foremen.
And leaving t'lass to deal with Dostoevsky.

I know the North that thrums its belts and engines
Brandishing its realism and squalor
Its heavy woollen facts of wealth and power,
Wealth and Power my eye,

Tuppeny ha'penny tycoons with weak bladders
And dehydrating lemonading socialism.

I know the North
Its grey faces, closed theatres and stinking shops.
I know the cold wind, the provincial cant.
The football pools sing happy land in Preston
– And it's true that people dress better in London
And the football here is wilder and more local
And when you get up to Scotland the crowds are always
     fighting
Rangers v Celtic broken bottles red hair and floods of drunks.

I feel more at home watching Hull Kingston Rovers
And pretending to understand working men
(In one of those clean pubs on the housing estate)
Than sitting on a tatty night club on the Left Bank
With Gregory Corso or somebody
Listening to a lot of political satire
In a language I don't understand. . . .

BRIAN HIGGINS

Birmingham*

Auschwitz with H and C
Seven a.m. and vacuum cleaners
at full throttle. Brum Brum Brum.
Grey curtains against a grey sky
Wall to wall linoleum and the
ashtray nailed to the mantlepiece.
Sacrificing breakfast for semidreams
I remember the days we stayed
at the Albany. Five Ten a night.
I was somebody then (the one on the right
with glasses singing Lily the Pink).
The Dolce Vita.

At 10. o'clock the Kommodante
(a thin spinster, prim as shrapnel)
balls me out of bed. 'Get up
or I'll fetch the police. Got guests
arriving at midday. Businessmen.
This room's to be cleaned and ready.'
  i Kleenextissues to be uncrumpled and ironed
 ii Dust reassembled
iii Fresh nail in the ashtray
iv Harpic down the plughole
  v Beds to be seen and not aired.

*This comes from a collection of poems about a musical group travelling
around the country.

In the lounge my fellow refugees
are cowering together for warmth.
**No gas fires allowed before 6.30
in the evening. Verboten.**
We draw straws. The loser
rings the service bell. 'Tea! Tea!!
I've got more to do than run around
making tea at all hours of the day.

Tea!!!' She goosesteps down the hall.
A strange quirk of feet.
When the bill comes there is
included a 12½% service charge.
We tell her to stick it
up her brum. La dolce vita.

ROGER McGOUGH

The Oxford Voice

When you hear it languishing
and hooing and cooing and sidling through the front teeth,
　　　　the oxford voice
　　　　or worse still
　　　　the would–be oxford voice
you don't even laugh any more, you can't.
For every blooming bird is an oxford cuckoo nowadays,
you can't sit on a bus nor in the tube
but it breathes gently and languishingly in the back of your
　neck.

And oh, so seductively superior, so seductively
　　　　self–effacingly
　　　　deprecatingly
　　　　superior. –
We wouldn't insist on it for a moment
　　　　but we are
　　　　　we are
　　　　you admit we are
　　　　　superior.—

D. H. LAWRENCE

'Gentlemen'*

God placed the Russian peasant
Under the Great White Czar;
God put the Prussian worker
Beneath the Lord of War.
But he sent the English gentleman,
The perfect English gentleman,
God's own good English gentleman,
To make us what we are.

Our fathers once were freemen,
And as freemen wont to toil,
To reap the fruitful harvest,
And to gather golden spoil.
But the greedy, grasping gentlemen,
The land-engrossing gentlemen,
The honest English gentlemen,
They stole away the soil.

They drove us from our villages
By force and fraud and stealth,
They drove us into factories,
They robbed us of our health.
But the cotton-spinning gentlemen,
The coal-mine, shipyard gentlemen,
Stockbroking, banking gentlemen,
They gathered wondrous wealth.

We toil to make them prosperous,
We fight to make them great;
But we know how they have robbed us,
We bide our time and wait:
While the fat, well-living gentlemen,
The easy, well-bred gentlemen,
The thoughtless, careless gentlemen,
Forget that slaves can hate.

*This sharp attack appeared in an anthology entitled *Poems of Revolt* which
was published in 1924 by the Labour Publishing Company.

The patient Russian peasant
Has turned and smashed his Czar;
Some day the Prussian worker
Will break his Lord of War.
And soon – ah! soon, our gentlemen,
Our proud, all-powerful gentlemen,
Our God-damned English gentlemen,
Shall find out what we are.

W. N. EWER

County

God save me from the Porkers,
    God save me from their sons,
Their noisy tweedy sisters
    Who follow with the guns,
The old and scheming mother,
    Their futures that she plann'd,
The ghastly younger brother
    Who married into land.

Their shots along the valley
    Draw blood out of the sky,
The wounded pheasants rally
    As hobnailed boots go by.
Where once the rabbit scampered
    The waiting copse is still
As Porker fat and pampered
    Comes puffing up the hill.

'A left and right! Well done, sir!
    They're falling in the road;
And here's your other gun, sir.'
    'Don't talk. You're here to load.'
He grabs his gun, not seeing
    A thing but birds in air,
And blows them out of being
    With self-indulgent stare.

Triumphant after shooting
    He still commands the scene,
His Land Rover comes hooting
    Beaters and dogs between.
Then dinner with a neighbour,
    It doesn't matter which,
Conservative or Labour,
    So long as he is rich.

A *faux-bonhomme* and dull as well,
    All pedigree and purse,
We must admit that, though he's hell,
    His womenfolk are worse.
Bright in their county gin sets
    They tug their ropes of pearls
And smooth their tailored twin-sets
    And drop the names of earls.

Loud talks of meets and marriages
    And tax-evasion's heard
In many first-class carriages
    While servants travel third.
'My dear, I have to spoil them too –
    Or who would do the chores?
Well, here we are at Waterloo,
    I'll drop you at the Stores.'

God save me from the Porkers,
    The pathos of their lives,
The strange example that they set
    To new-rich farmers' wives
Glad to accept their bounty
    And worship from afar,
And think of them as county –
    County is what they are.

JOHN BETJEMAN

And Hate My Next-Door Neighbour

The World State

Oh, how I love Humanity,
    With love so pure and pringlish,
And how I hate the horrid French,
    Who never will be English!

The International Idea,
    The largest and the clearest,
Is welding all the nations now,
    Except the one that's nearest.

This compromise has long been known,
    This scheme of partial pardons,
In ethical societies
    And small suburban gardens –

The villas and the chapels where
    I learned with little labour
The way to love my fellow-man
    And hate my next-door neighbour.

                    G. K. CHESTERTON

On Dublin*

Sometimes you brought invective down
Upon the 'blind and ignorant town'
Which I would half disclaim;
For in my laughing heart I knew
Its scheming and demeaning crew
Was useful as the opposite to
The mood that leads to fame;

*Boss Croker was a Tammany politician who won the Derby with an Irish
horse. Dublin gave him the freedom of the city, but refused to honour Yeats
in this way. The British Ambassador now lives in Croker's rambling Gothic
mansion in the outskirts of Dublin.

For very helpful is the town
Where we by contradicting come
Much nearer to our native home;
But yet it made me grieve
To think its mounted-beggar race
Makes Dublin the most famous place
For famous men to leave:
Where City Fathers staged a farce
And honoured one who owned a horse;
They win right well our sneers
Who of their son took no account
Though he had Pegasus to mount
And rode two hemispheres.
Return Dean Swift, and elevate
Our townsmen to the equine state!

OLIVER ST JOHN GOGARTY
from *Elegy on the Archpoet
William Butler Yeats Lately Dead*

On France

OH BLAST FRANCE
      PIG PLAGIARISM
      BELLY
      SLIPPERS
      POODLE TEMPER
      BAD MUSIC
SENTIMENTAL GALLIC GUSH
      SENSATIONALISM
      FUSSINESS
      PARISIAN PAROCHIALISM

WYNDHAM LEWIS
from *Blast*

On America

America I've given you all and now I'm nothing.
America two dollars and twentyseven cents January 17, 1956.
I can't stand on my own mind.
America when will we end the human war?
Go fuck yourself with your atom bomb.
I don't feel good don't bother me.
I won't write my poem till I'm in my right mind.
America when will you be angelic?
When will you take off your clothes?
When will you look at yourself through the grave?
When will you be worthy of your million Trotskyites?
America why are your libraries full of tears?
America when will you send your eggs to India?
I'm sick of your insane demands.
When can I go into the supermarket and buy what I need
    with my good looks?
America after all it is you and I who are perfect not the next
    world.
Your machinery is too much for me.
You made me want to be a saint.
There must be some other way to settle this argument. . . .

ALLEN GINSBERG
from *America*

The Reason

A rather extreme vegetarian,
Looked down from his summit Bavarian,
    He said: 'It's not odd
    I'm superior to God,
For the Latter's not even an Aryan.'

SAGITTARIUS

71

Arabesque*

Now tidings of Arab unrest dismay connoisseurs in the West.
Aggressions too sternly repressed result in extreme
  hypertension.
The kith by the kin are pursued, vendetta and vengeance
  renewed,
But it's only a family feud; no need the Israelis to mention.

But it means an unholy Jehad when Arab relations are bad,
No peace from Beirut to Baghdad, no truce for the States that
  were Trucial.
When in-laws and outlaws disperse, exchanging the family
  curse,
The mess that was Mespot gets worse, and the crisis for
  Cairo more crucial.

But O, for the Cup by the pool that made captive Emirs keep
  cool
When under the yoke of Stamboul condemned to luxurious
  leisure!
For the Princes made terms with the Porte for a
  Bashi-Bazouki escort,
Conducting art-lovers to Court in palaces bursting with
  treasure.

Confirmed in their Tourist Rights, all offered Arabian Nights
With Persian and Turkish Delights, and Iran went shares
  with Iraq.
And the guest from the West in Islam breathed a climate of
  cultural calm,
And proud Sheikhs made stately salaam, salaaming to Miss
  Freya Stark.

*Sagittarius is the pseudonym of Olga Katzin who wrote a weekly parody
for the New Statesman in the 1930's and the 1940's. She is still rhyming and
sent to me this more contemporary piece, which is based on one of Flecker's
poems. The other poems by her in this anthology first appeared in the New
Statesman, as did the poems by Roger Woddis who has succeeded her as their
regular poetical commentator. Together, they have created over the years
the sharpest poetical column in journalism.

None panted for battles to come, none pined for the trumpet
and drum,
The cavalry camels were glum, the falcons dejectedly
moulting.
But who fanned the passions of war! Who roused Arab
esprit-de-corps,
Till revolt in the desert they swore, and have never since then
ceased revolting?

We have Lawrence ben Lawrence to thank, who triggered the
Bedouin prank,
That Anglo-Arabian swank who drove them completely
berserk.
But as for Fine Arts and *Belles Lettres*, silks, carpets, ceramics,
etcetera,
Well, things were a jolly sight betterer in the days of the
Terrible Turk!

SAGITTARIUS

I Wanna Go Back To Dixie

I wanna go back to Dixie,
Take me back to dear ol' Dixie,
That's the only li'l ol' place for li'l ol' me.

Old times there are not forgotten,
Whuppin' slaves and sellin' cotton,
And waitin' for the Robert E. Lee.
(It was never there on time.)

I'll go back to the Swanee,
Where pellagra makes you scrawny,
And the honeysuckle clutters up the vine.

I really am a fixin'
To go home and start a mixin'
Down below that Mason Dixon line.

I wanna go back to Alabammy,
Back to the arms of my dear ol' Mammy,
Her cookin's lousy and her hands are clammy,
But what the hell, it's home.

Yes, for paradise the Southland is my nominee.

Just give me a hamhock and a grit of hominy.

I wanna go back to Dixie,
I wanna be a Dixie pixie
And eat corn pone till it's comin' out of my ears.
I wanna talk with southern gentlemen
And put my white sheet on again,
I ain't seen one good lynchin' in years.
The land of the boll weevil,
Where the laws are medieval,
Is callin' me to come and never more roam –

I wanna go back to the Southland,
That y' all and 'shet ma mouth' land.
Be it ever so decadent,
There's no place like home.

TOM LEHRER

A Colonist In His Garden*

Write not that you content can be,
Pent by that drear and shipless sea
Round lonely islands rolled,
Isles nigh as empty as their deep,
Where men but talk of gold and sheep
And think of sheep and gold.

*These are the words put into the mouth of an English settler in New
Zealand by the New Zealand politician and poet William Pember Reeves in
1904. He'd been a member of the great reforming Liberal Cabinet in the
1880's, but he moved to London where he found the Fabian circles more
congenial. He declined to become a British M. P. in 1899 but he did become
the Director of the London School of Economics. His most significant
monument is the New Zealand weekend, which makes the English Sunday
look like a Bacchanalian festival. His Shops Act made shops close on Friday
evenings and open on Monday mornings and they still do.

A land without a past; a race
Set in the rut of commonplace;
Where Demos overfed
Allows no gulf, respects no height;
And grace and colour, music, light,
From sturdy scorn are fled.

WILLIAM PEMBER REEVES

To A Russian Soldier In Prague

You are going to be hated by the people.

They will hate you over their freakish breakfast of tripe soup
and pastries.
They will squint hatred at you on their way to pretend to
work.
By the light of yellow beer they will hate you with jokes
you'll never hear.

You're beginning to feel
Like a landlord in a slum
Like a white man in Harlem
Like a U.S. Marine in Saigon

Socialists are hated
By all who kill for profit and power.
But you are going to be hated by
The people – who are all different.
The people – who are all extraordinary.
The people – who are all of equal value.
Socialism is theirs, it was invented for them.
Socialism is theirs, it can only be made by them.

Africa, Asia and Latin America are screaming:
STARVATION. POVERTY. OPPRESSION.
When they turn to America
They see only flames and children in the flames.

75

When they turn to England
They see an old lady in a golden wheelchair,
Share certificates in one hand, a pistol in the other.
When they turn to Russia
They see – you.

You are going to be hated
As the English have usually been hated.
The starving, the poor and the oppressed
Are turning, turning away.
While you nervously guard a heap of documents
They stagger away through the global crossfire
Towards revolution, towards socialism.

ADRIAN MITCHELL

Scotland The Wee

Scotland the wee, crèche of the soul,
of thee I sing

land of the millionaire draper, whisky vomit
and the Hillman Imp

staked out with church halls, gaelic sangs
and the pan loaf

eventide home for teachers and christians,
nirvana of the keelie imagination

Stenhousemuir, Glenrothes, Auchterarder, Renton
– one way street to the coup of the mind.

TOM BUCHAN

Let The Day Perish
Wherein I Was Born

On Man*

Be Judge your self, I'll bring it to the test,
Which is the basest creature man, or beast?
Birds, feed on birds, beasts, on each other prey,
But savage man alone, does man, betray:
Prest by necessity they kill for food,
Man, undoes man, to do himself no good.
With teeth, and claws by Nature arm'd they hunt,
Natures allowances, to supply their want.
But man, with smiles, embraces, friendships, praise,
Unhumanely his fellows life betrays;
With voluntary pains, works his distress,
Not through necessity, but wantonness.
For hunger, or for love, they fight or tear,
Whilst wretched man, is still in arms for fear;
For fear he armes, and is of armes afraid,
By fear, to fear, successively betray'd
Base fear, the source whence his best passion came,
His boasted honor, and his dear bought fame.

The good he acts, the ill he does endure,
'Tis all for fear, to make himself secure.
Meerly for safety, after fame we thirst,
For all men, would be cowards if they durst.

JOHN WILMOT,
EARL OF ROCHESTER
from *A Satire Against Mankind*

*Before he was twenty Rochester was one of the most famous of the Restoration rakes. Much of his life was spent in a drunken haze and he died from pox at the age of 32. He was a fine satirist and poet; Voltaire called him a great one. When he was thirty years old he described himself in a letter to a friend as 'almost blind, utterly lame, and scarce within the reasonable hopes of ever seeing London again'.

Resumé*

Razors pain you;
Rivers are damp;
Acids stain you;
And drugs cause cramp.
Guns aren't lawful;
Nooses give;
Gas smells awful
You might as well live.

DOROTHY PARKER

On Old Age**

Mistaken blessing, which old age they call,
T'is a long, nasty, darksome hospital,
A ropey chain of rhumes; a visage rough,
Deformed, unfeatured, and a skin of buff.
A stitch-fallen cheek, that hangs below the jaw;
Such wrinkles as a skilful hand would draw
For an old grandam ape, when, with a grace,
She sits at squat, and scrubs her leathern face.

The skull and forehead one bold barren plain;
And gums unarmed to mumble meat in vain:
Besides the eternal drivel that supplies
The dropping beard, from nostrils, mouth and eyes.
His wife and children loathe him, and, what's worse
Himself does his offensive carrion curse!
What music or enchanting voice can chear
A stupid, old, impenetrable ear?

JOHN DRYDEN
from *Juvenal's Sixth Satire*

* Dorothy Parker wrote frequently with a sense of 'ennui' and occasionally with real distaste for life. But she outlived most of the rest of the world-weary and witty set that met at the Algonquin Hotel, New York, in the twenties and thirties. When she died at the age of 73 in 1967 many people were surprised to know that she had survived for so long.

** This was written by Juvenal about A.D. 120 and translated by Dryden in 1693. As the geriatric wards grow larger is their picture less true of today?

Job Complaineth Of Life

After this opened Job his mouth, and cursed his day.

And Job spake, and said,

Let the day perish wherein I was born, and the night in which it was said, There is a man child conceived.

Let that day be darkness; let not God regard it from above, neither let the light shine upon it; let darkness and the shadow of death stain it; let a cloud dwell upon it; let the blackness of the day terrify it.

As for that night, let darkness seize upon it; let it not be joined unto the days of the year, let it not come into the number of the months.

Lo, let that night be solitary, let no joyful voice come therein.

Let them curse it that curse the day, who are ready to raise up their mourning.

Let the stars of the twilight thereof be dark; let it look for light, but have none; neither let it see the dawning of the day:

Because it shut not up the doors of my mother's womb, nor hid sorrow from mine eyes.

Why died I not from the womb? Why did I not give up the ghost when I came out of the belly?

Why did the knees prevent me? or why the breasts that I should suck?

For now should I have lain still and been quiet, I should have slept: then had I been at rest.

With kings and counsellors of the earth, which built desolate places for themselves;

Or with princes that had gold, who filled their houses with silver:

Or as an hidden untimely birth I had not been; as infants which never saw light.

There the wicked cease from troubling; and there the weary be at rest.

There the prisoners rest together; they hear not the voice of the oppressor.

The small and great are there; and the servant is free from his master.

81

Wherefore is light given to him that is in misery, and life
unto the bitter in soul;
   Which long for death, but it cometh not; and dig for it more
than for hid treasures;
   Which rejoice exceedingly, and are glad, when they can find
the grave?
   ... I was not in safety, neither had I rest, neither was I quiet,
yet trouble came.

from *The Authorized Version, Job, Chapter 3*

Sonnet XXIX

The world's a stage. The light is in one's eyes.
The Auditorium is extremely dark.
The more dishonest get the larger rise;
The more offensive make the greater mark.
The women on it prosper by their shape,
Some few by their vivacity. The men,
By tailoring in breeches and in cape.
The world's a stage – I say it once again.

The scenery is very much the best
Of what the wretched drama has to show,
Also the prompter happens to be dumb.
We drink behind the scenes and pass a jest
On all our folly; then, before we go
Loud cries for 'Author'... but he doesn't come.

HILAIRE BELLOC

Thoughts At Midnight

Mankind, you dismay me
When shadows waylay me! –
Not by your splendours
Do you affray me,
Not as pretenders

82

To demonic keenness
Not by your meanness,
Nor your ill-teachings,
Nor your false preachings,
Nor your banalities
And immoralities,
Nor by your daring
Nor sinister bearing;
But by your madnesses
Capping cool badnesses,
Acting like puppets
Under Time's buffets;
In superstitions
And ambitions
Moved by no wisdom,
Far-sight, or system,
Led by sheer senselessness
And presciencelessness
Into unreason
And hideous self-treason...
God, look he on you,
Have mercy upon you!

THOMAS HARDY

On Fame

So much the thirst of honour fires the blood
So many would be great, so few be good.
For who would virtue for herself regard,
Or wed, without the portion of reward?
Yet this mad chase of fame, by few pursued,
Has drawn destruction on the multitude:
This avarice of praise in times to come,
Those long inscriptions, crowded on the tomb,
Should some wild fig tree take her native bent,
And heave below the gaudy monument,

Would crack the marble titles, and disperse
The characters of all the lying verse.
For sepulchres themselves must crumbling fall
In times abyss, the common grave of all.

JOHN DRYDEN
from *Juvenal's Tenth Satire*

*There's No First Class To Heaven**

Have you got your tickets?
Have you got your furs?
Step into the bar and meet the other passengers,
All the folks are cheering on the quay
But the stewards look rather fishy and their manner's
     rather free,
It doesn't seem at all like pleasure cruising.

You may buy your way to a Tatler success
By the sit of your eyebrows, the cut of your dress,
But you can't grease the slipway to Happiness,
     There's no first class to Heaven.

You may score full marks by your fashion-plate hips,
Dorchester teeth or advertisement lips,
But you can't bribe Charon – he doesn't take tips,
     There's no first class to Heaven.

Goodbye limousine, milk and honeyland,
Soon there'll be an end, silk and moneyland,
Goodbye caviare, cars and Claridges,
Goodbye lovers and goodbye marriages.
     (Marriages are made in Heaven)

*Pennethorne Hughes was a master at Oundle school and later worked in
Bristol for the Talks Department of the BBC which sent him to Egypt in
1947. A selection of his poems was published by Geoffrey Grigson in 1970
and John Betjeman contributed a foreword as Pennethorne Hughes had
done much to popularise his poems on the BBC. The Pennethornes were the
children of George IV and Mrs John Nash.

Though you follow the fashion from Goodwood to Cannes
In eternal pursuit of the *live*-year plan,
You can't cheat that one-way ferryman,
    There's no first class to Heaven!

    Who has seen my valet?
    Is my luggage in the hold?
    There doesn't seem much service and it's really very cold,
    Look at those odd people on the deck,
    The captain can't talk English and he will not change my
      cheque,
    Tell me now why did we come along?
    Listen what a dreary note that gloomy landing gong!

You may buy your way to a paragraph fame
By your Cartier bills and your grandfather's name,
But you can't buy Peter – he isn't the same,
    There's no first class to Heaven.

You may get front seats for the best of the fun
At Polo or Lords or the new Cresta run.
When it comes to the end, though, you've only begun,
    There's no first class to Heaven.

Goodbye manicure, modes and Molyneux's,
Soon you'll have to pay all your folly dues,
Goodbye kisses in quiet localities
Where no chaperone, maid, or valet is.
    (You gotta behave in Heaven)

All those Embassy girls of notorious charm
Will still get their dancing: no need for alarm,
But it's hard to fox-trot to a harp and a psalm,
    There's no first class to Heaven!

                    PENNETHORNE HUGHES

Elderly Discontented Women

Elderly discontented women ask for intimate
    companionship,
by which they mean more talk, talk, talk
especially about themselves and their own feelings.

Elderly discontented women are so full of themselves
they have high blood-pressure and almost burst.

It is as if modern women had all got themselves on the brain
and that sent the blood rushing to the surface of the body
and driving them around in frenzied energy
stampeding over everybody,
while their hearts become absolutely empty,
and their voices are like screw-drivers
as they try to screw everybody else down with their will.

D. H. LAWRENCE

Mother Nature's Bloomers

See Mother Nature's bloomers here! –
    A pretty hopeless crew, sir…
Who are this mob? I greatly fear
    They're you, madame, and you, sir!

You'd think the dear old girl would see
    It's time to stop and wonder
For mortal man's turned out to be
    Her most appalling blunder.

    Mother Nature's bloomers
    Mother Nature's bloomers
    Mother Nature's bloomers
        They're you, madame, and you, sir!

86

In time no doubt she'll glumly say
    'This lot could not be wetter'.
She'll scrap us all and start next day
    With something rather better.

But till at last she tries her luck
    With peewits, pike or pumas,
The world is stuck – the world is stuck!
    With Mother Nature's bloomers.

LEONARD BARRAS

The Wicked Grocer Groces . . .

The Devil's Thoughts

From his brimstone bed at break of day
A walking the Devil is gone,
To visit his snug little farm the earth,
And see how his stock goes on.

Over the hill and over the dale,
And he went over the plain,
And backward and forward he switched his long tail
As a gentleman switches his cane.

And how then was the Devil drest?
Oh! he was in his Sunday's best:
His jacket was red and his breeches were blue,
And there was a hole where the tail came through.

He saw a Lawyer killing a Viper
On a dunghill hard by his own stable;
And the Devil smiled, for it put him in mind
Of Cain and his brother, Abel.

He saw an Apothecary on a white horse
    Ride by on his vocations,
And the Devil thought of his old Friend
    Death in the Revelations.

He saw a cottage with a double coach-house,
    A cottage of gentility;
And the Devil did grin, for his darling sin
    Is pride that apes humility. . . .

SAMUEL TAYLOR COLERIDGE

On A Civil Servant

Here lies a civil servant. He was civil
To everyone, and servant to the devil.

C. H. SISSON

The Lawyer

A fox may steal your hens, Sir,
A trull your health and pence, Sir,
Your daughter may rob your chest, Sir,
Your wife may steal your rest, Sir,
  A thief your goods and plate.

But this is all but picking,
With rest, pence, chest, and chicken;
It ever was decreed, Sir,
If Lawyer's hand is fee'd, Sir,
  He steals your whole estate.

JOHN GAY

A Judge Commits Suicide

A Judge has sentenced himself to a suicide's grave?
– The nearest to a just sentence any judge ever gave.

HUGH MacDIARMID

The Justice Of The Peace

Distinguish carefully between these two,
  This thing is yours, that other thing is mine.
You have a shirt, a brimless hat, a shoe
  And half a coat. I am the Lord benign
Of fifty hundred acres of fat land
To which I have a right. You understand?

I have a right because I have, because,
  Because I have – because I have a right.
Now be quite calm and good, obey the laws,
  Remember your low station, do not fight
Against the goad, because, you know, it pricks
Whenever the uncleanly demos kicks.

I do not envy you your hat, your shoe.
    Why should you envy me my small estate?
It's fearfully illogical in you
    To fight with economic force and fate.
Moreover, I have got the upper hand,
And mean to keep it. Do you understand?

HILAIRE BELLOC

The Song Against Grocers

God made the wicked Grocer
For a mystery and a sign,
That men might shun the awful shops
And go to inns to dine;
Where the bacon's on the rafter
And the wine is in the wood,
And God that made good laughter
Has seen that they are good.

The evil-hearted Grocer
Would call his mother 'Ma'am',
And bow at her and bob at her,
Her aged soul to damn,
And rub his horrid hands and ask
What article was next,
Though *mortis in articulo*
Should be her proper text.

His props are not his children,
But pert lads underpaid,
Who call out 'Cash!' and bang about
To work his wicked trade;
He keeps a lady in a cage
Most cruelly all day,
And makes her count and calls her 'Miss'
Until she fades away.

The righteous minds of innkeepers
Induce them now and then
To crack a bottle with a friend
Or treat unmoneyed men,
But who hath seen the Grocer
Treat housemaids to his teas
Or crack a bottle of fish-sauce
Or stand a man a cheese!

He sells us sands of Araby
As sugar for cash down;
He sweeps his shop and sells the dust
The purest salt in town,
He crams with cans of poisoned meat
Poor subjects of the King,
And when they die by thousands
Why, he laughs like anything.

The wicked Grocer groces
In spirits and in wine,
Not frankly and in fellowship
As men in inns do dine;
But packed with soap and sardines
And carried off by grooms,
For to be snatched by Duchesses
And drunk in dressing-rooms.

The hell-instructed Grocer
Has a temple made of tin,
And the ruin of good innkeepers
Is loudly urged therein;
But now the sands are running out
From sugar of a sort,
The Grocer trembles; for his time,
Just like his weight, is short.

G. K. CHESTERTON

The General (1917)

'Good morning – good morning!' the General said
When we met him last week on our way to the Line
Now the soldiers he smiled at are most of 'em dead,
And we're cursing his staff for incompetent swine.
'He's a cheery old card' grunted Harry to Jack
As they slogged up to Arras with rifle and pack.
But he did for them both with his plan of attack.

SIEGFRIED SASSOON

A Wish

Nor bring, to see me cease to live,
Some doctor full of phrase and fame,
To shake his sapient head, and give
The ill he cannot cure a name.

MATTHEW ARNOLD

On Critics*

'Critics! appall'd I venture on the name,
Those cut-throat bandits in the path of fame,
Bloody dissectors, worse than ten Monroes:
He hacks to teach, they mangle to expose:
By blockhead's daring into madness stung,
His heart by wanton, causeless malice wrung,
His well-worn bays – than life itself more dear –
By miscreants torn, who ne'er one sprig must wear;
Foil'd, bleeding, tortur'd in th' unequal strife,
The hapless Poet flounces on through life,
Till, fled each Muse that glorious once inspir'd,

*Scottish poets have always seemed to be over-sensitive to criticism. Two centuries later Hugh MacDiarmid had this to say about English critics: 'The majority of literary critics, especially London ones, recall to me that extraordinary chirruping conversation which sounds almost human but, on investigation with an electric torch, is found to be merely a couple of hedgehogs courting beneath one's window.'

Low-sunk in squalid, unprotected age,
Dead even resentment for his injur'd page,
He heeds no more the ruthless critics rage.
　So by some hedge the generous steed deceas'd,
For half-starv'd, snarling curs a dainty feast:
By toil and famine worn to skin and bone,
Lies, senseless of each tugging bitch's son.'

ROBERT BURNS
from *The Poet's Progress*

Pop Sociologist

Professor Klaxon, mod in style,
Was a hustler.
He visited prisons but rarely voted;
'Barrios and bullets, not ballots, are my bag',
He said at one party.
He wore peon clothes, but not their politeness.
Bearded and bulgy,
He oozed like a hippy through heists
Of Federal, State, and Local Funds –
A new Laocoon, entwined in tapes
Of ghetto speech and governors of prisons.
Raucous, raunchy, but REAL, man!
(Do not speak of Sociology to him.)
　　　Through his intuitive sympathy
　　　With prisoners and wardens
　　　His archives housed convict songs,
　　　Conversations with con-men,
　　　And, of course,
　　　'Which Side Are You On?'
And while he puffs his pipe
(Reeking of the best Latakia)
And plays his records
On diamond needles,
The people he records
Dig silver needles into their arms,
They too desiring some distance from the truth.

J. P. SULLIVAN

On Authors And Publishers

What authors lose, their booksellers have won,
So pimps grow rich, while gallants are undone.

ALEXANDER POPE

My Five Gentlemen*

Prostitutes have clients, wives have husbands,
Poets, you will understand, have editors.
A mediaeval saint had lice which quietly left him
As his body cooled, their sustenance removed from them.

I have my five gentlemen, one of whom really was
A gentle man, courteous and kind, his rejection slips
Even appeared to be some kind of acceptance,
His face never seen, his care meticulous and honest.

Two was firm and neatly pruned my lines
Like a competent gardener tidying an unwieldy tree.
Faced with mis-spelt, badly typed pages,
He was even provoked into swearing mildly at me.

Three was a witty man, who wrote letters
On a kind of elegant toilet paper, and seen
At a party looked as practised at his social life
As he was at his poetry, though thickening a little.

---

* Elizabeth Bartlett writes of herself 'I was born of working class parents near
the Kent coalfields in 1923. My father was an ex-sergeant in the army and my
mother a house-parlourmaid. Educated at an elementary school, I won a
scholarship to grammar school, only to be removed at the age of 15 to work
in a hypodermic needle factory. I started writing poetry at school and was
first published at the age of 19. I cannot explain a life-long passion for this
private art.' Her first collection *A Lifetime of Dying* was published in 1979.

Four was a shocking surprise. He was not at all
Pretentious. Squinting furtively at him, silent and wary,
I saw this pleasant face, heard a quiet voice, and saw him
Lasting more than a decade or two, a rare animal.

Five is dead, of course. His failing health
Was a comfort to me, though not to him,
Naturally. His death removed one more market
For battered goods, and proved a welcome release.

Rest in peace, I thought (for I always think kindly
Of the gentlemen who direct me to the pages
I am to sit in). I can only hope to be re-cycled
And end up more useful than I would appear to be.

ELIZABETH BARTLETT

On Lord Mayors*

Innumerable City knights we know
From Blue-coat Hospitals and Bridewells flow.
Draymen and porters fill the city chair,
And footboys magisterial purple wear.
Fate has but very small distinction set
Betwixt the counter and the coronet...
Great families of yesterday we show,
And lords, whose parents were the Lord knows who.

DANIEL DEFOE
from *The True-born Englishman*

*Many people want to be Lord Mayor of London although they have to find
£50,000 from their own pocket for this honour. Max Beerbohm had no
doubts about this strange ambition for when he was a theatre critic he had
this to say of a production of *Dick Whittington*: 'On Highgate Hill, that
depressing spot, he sinks down on a stone and dreams that he is to be Lord
Mayor of London. This horrible and vulgar destiny haunts him throughout
his chequered career, till at last it is actually fulfilled.'

a salesman

a salesman is an it that stinks Excuse

Me whether it's president of the you were say
or a jennelman name misder finger isn't
important whether it's millions of other punks
or just a handful absolutely doesn't
matter and whether it's in lonejewray

or shrouds is immaterial it stinks

a salesman is an it that stinks to please

but whether to please itself or someone else
makes no more difference than if it sells
hate condoms education snakeoil vac
uumcleaners terror strawberries democ
ra (caveat emptor) cy superflous hair

or Think We've Met subhuman rights Before

e. e. cummings

The Passport Officer

This impartial dog's nose
scrutinizes the lamppost. All in good order.
He sets his seal on it and
moves on to the next.

(The drippings of his forerunners
convey no information,
barely a precedent.
His actions are reflex.)

BASIL BUNTING

Sensation*

Yellow and poster-striped the hornet vans
swarm into view hymning Humanity,
Truth, and the Public Good – their glands
charged with the venom to infect a city.

                    JON STALLWORTHY

The British Journalist

You cannot hope
    to bribe or twist,
thank God! the
    British journalist.

But, seeing what
    the man will do
unbribed, there's
    no occasion to.

                    HUMBERT WOLFE

On The Times

Let us deride the smugness of 'The Times':
GUFFAW!
So much the gagged reviewers,
It will pay them when the worms are wriggling in their
    vitals;
These were they who objected to newness,
HERE are their TOMB-STONES.
They supported the gag and the ring;

---

*This was written in Summer 1963 – the long hot summer of the Profumo
crisis. The crisis had all the ingredients that the popular press liked – call girls,
a Minister of the Crown, spies and lavish parties. The drama was revealed
with slow relish. Profumo was disgraced; Christine Keeler was briefly
imprisoned, and Dr Ward committed suicide, leaving beside his body the
plaintive note 'Delay Resuscitation.'

A little black box contains them.
So shall you be also,
You slut-bellied obstructionist;
You sworn foe to free speech and good letters,
You fungus, you continuous gangrene. . . .
I have seen many who go about with supplications,
Afraid to say how they hate you.
HERE is the taste of my BOOT,
CARESS it, lick off the BLACKING.

WYNDHAM LEWIS
from *Blast* (1914)

The London Zoo

From one of the cages on the periphery
He is brought to London, but only for duty.
As if radio-controlled he comes without a keeper,
Without any resistance, five times in the week.
See him as he rises in his ordered household,
Docile each morning before he is expelled,
Take his bath when he is told, use the right towel,
Reliable as an ant, meticulous as an owl.
His wife, until he is gone, is anxiously protective
In case after all one morning he should resist,
But all is well each day, he hasn't the spirit
– He is edged out of the door without even a murmur.
The road to the station is reassuring
For other black hats are doing the same thing
Some striding blithely who were never athletic,
Others, who were, now encased in Cadillacs,
Smug and still belching from their breakfast bacon,
All, halt and well, keen to be on the train.

Each sits by other whom a long acquaintance
Has made familiar as a chronic complaint,
Although the carapaces they wear are so thick
That the tender souls inside are far to seek.

First there is *The Times* newspaper, held before the eyes
As an outer defence and a guarantee of propriety,
Then the clothes which are not entirely uniform
So as to give the appearance of a personal epidermis,
But most resistant of all is the layer of language
Swathed around their senses like a mile of bandage;
Almost nothing gets in through that, but when something
    does,
The answering thought squelches out like pus. . . .

Out on the platform like money from a cashier's shovel
The responsible people fall at the end of their travel.
Some are indignant that their well-known faces
Are not accepted instead of railway passes;
Others faithfully produce the card by which the authorities
Regulate the movement of animals in great cities.
With growing consciousness of important function
Each man sets out for where he is admired most,
The one room in London where everything is arranged
To enlarge his importance and deaden his senses.
The secretary who awaits him has corrected her bosom;
His papers are in the disorder he has chosen.
Anxieties enough to blot out consciousness
Are waiting satisfactorily upon his desk. . . .

C. H. SISSON

The Ways Of God Are Strange

Verses Written Upon Windows

The Church and clergy here, no doubt,
    Are very near a-kin;
Both, weather-beaten are without;
    And empty both within.

JONATHAN SWIFT

In Church

'And now to God the Father,' he ends,
And his voice thrills up to the topmost tiles:
Each listener chokes as he bows and bends,
And emotion pervades the crowded aisles.
Then the preacher glides to the vestry-door,
And shuts it, and thinks he is seen no more.

The door swings softly ajar meanwhile,
And a pupil of his in the Bible class,
Who adores him as one without gloss or guile,
Sees her idol stand with a satisfied smile
And re-enact at the vestry-glass
Each pulpit gesture in deft dumb-show
That had moved the congregation so.

THOMAS HARDY

Nuts In May

I saw twa items on
The T.V. programme yesterday.
'General Assembly of the Church of Scotland'
Said ane – the ither 'Nuts in May.'
I lookit at the picters syne
But which was which I couldna say.

HUGH MacDIARMID

For Canon Brown,
Who Likes Contemporary Speech*

Do not imagine, Canon Brown,
That when the chips are really down
It will be folk like you who speak
So plain, while we are sham antique.
Do you know, arrogant old fool,
(That's modern, mate, so keep your cool)
It is you who are antiquarian
And we who think that san ne fairy-ann
Whether the words are old or new
But only, what work they can do?
What work can you do, idle lump?
While you defile the parish pump
Some of us like our water clean
And like to use words we can *mean*.
And so did Cranmer, who had to cook
For standing by his common book.
Write me a Book of Common Prayer
That is not made up of hot air
With words that are as plain as this
And, oh boy! that will take the piss
Out of those who wrote Series 3
And (I confess it) out of me.

C. H. SISSON

---

*In the winter of 1979 the debate over the use of the Cranmer liturgy as opposed to the modern English version Series 3 came to a head. A pro-Cranmer petition was signed by 600 well-known people and a Canon Brown from Devizes wrote to *The Guardian*, saying that such matters should be left to the Church. This so incensed the poet C. H. Sisson that he wrote this poem and travelled to Devizes to pin it, like a latter-day Luther, to the door of Canon Brown's church. Alas the organist found it first and took it down. But it should not be lost to posterity.

Was It Not Curious?*

Was it not curious of Aúgustin
Saint Aúgustin, Saint Aúgustin,
When he saw the beautiful British children
To say such a curious thing?

He said he must send the gospel, the gospel,
At once to them over the waves
He never said he thought it was wicked
To steal them away for slaves

To steal the children away
To buy and have slavery at all
Oh no, oh no, it was not a thing
That caused him any appal.

Was it not curious of *Gregory*
Rather more than of Aúgustin?
It was not curious so much
As it was wicked of them.

STEVIE SMITH

'They'

The Bishop tells us: 'When the boys come back
They will not be the same; for they'll have fought
In a just cause: they lead the last attack
On Anti–Christ: their comrade's blood has bought
New right to breed an honourable race.
They have challenged Death and dared him face to face'.

---

*One of the most famous legends in English History centres on the comment that Gregory made when he saw young blond slaves from England being sold in the market place in Rome in the sixth century: 'They are not Angles, they are Angels.' This memory persuaded him when he became Pope to send Aúgustine to England to convert the Heathens to Christianity.

'We're none of us the same!' the boys reply.
'For George lost both his legs; and Bill's stone blind;
Poor Jim's shot through the lungs and like to die;
And Bert's gone syphilitic: you'll not find
A chap who's served that hasn't found some change.'
And the Bishop said: 'The ways of God are strange!'

SIEGFRIED SASSOON

A Moral Tale*
(After W. H. Auden)

'No one ever has the authority to destroy unborn life.' – *The Pope*.

Let me tell you a little story
　About Miss Edith Gee;
She lacked the kind of figure
　That decorates page 3.

She had narrow sloping shoulders
　And she had no bust at all,
But one evening on the common
　In fear she gave her all.

She did not love the stranger,
　She had to yield to force,
And more than her eyes were swollen
　As nature took its course.

She went to Doctor Brady,
　He rubbed his shaven chin;
'To do the thing you ask me
　Would be a mortal sin.'

*In October 1979 the Pope John Paul II made a triumphal progress through Ireland and the United States, addressing vast crowds, one of which in Ireland was estimated to consist of one third of the entire population. His Holiness took the opportunity to re-assert the traditional Catholic teachings against abortion and birth-control. Owing to his immense popular appeal and the authority that his physical appearance conveyed, few dared to challenge him. Not so Roger Woddis, who adapted Auden's poem, 'Miss Gee'.

And since he thought it sinful
   To end an unborn life,
She ended in a back street
   Beneath a rusty knife.

And now in Hell she suffers
   For all Eternity;
There never was a lady
   As wicked as Miss Gee.

ROGER WODDIS

All Things Dull And Ugly

All things dull and ugly
All creatures short and squat
All things rude and nasty
The Lord God made the lot.

Each little snake that poisons
Each little wasp that stings
He made their brutish venom
He made their horrid wings.

All things sick and cancerous
All evil great and small
All things foul and dangerous
The Lord God made them all.

Each nasty little hornet
Each beastly little squid
Who made the spikey urchin,
Who made the sharks? He did.

All things scabbed and ulcerous
All pox both great and small
Putrid, foul and gangrenous,
The Lord God made them all.

Amen.

MONTY PYTHON

Behold The Politician

On Irish Members Of Parliament

Let them, when they once get in,
Sell the nation for a pin;
While they sit a picking straws,
Let them rave at making laws,
While they never hold their tongue,
Let them dabble in their dung,
Let them form a grand committee,
How to plague and starve the city;
Let them stare, and storm, and frown,
When they see a clergy gown;
Let them, e'er they crack a louse,
Call for th'orders of the house;
Let them with their gosling quills
Scribble senseless heads of bills.
We may, while they strain their throats,
Wipe our a...s with their votes. . . .

JONATHAN SWIFT
from *The Legion Club*

On American Politicians

Behold the politician.
Self-preservation is his ambition.
He thrives in the D. of C.,
Where he was sent by you and me.

Whether elected or appointed
He considers himself the Lord's anointed,
And indeed the ointment lingers on him
So thick you can't get your fingers on him.

He has developed a sixth sense
About living at the public expense,
Because in private competition
He would encounter malnutrition.

113

He has many profitable hobbies
Not the least of which is lobbies.
He would not sell his grandmother for a quarter
If he suspected the presence of a reporter.

He gains votes ever and anew
By taking money from everybody and giving it to a few,
While explaining that every penny
Was extracted from the few to be given to the many.

Some politicians are Republican, some Democratic,
And their feud is dramatic,
But except for the name
They are identically the same.

ANON after OGDEN NASH

Epitaph On The Politician Himself

Here richly, with ridiculous display,
The Politician's corpse was laid away.
While all of his acquaintance sneered and slanged
I wept: for I had longed to see him hanged.

HILAIRE BELLOC

Oh To Be In England Now That Winston's Out*

Oh to be in England now that Winston's out
Now that there's room for doubt
And the bank may be the nation's
And the long years of patience
And labour's vacillations

*This little tirade appears in one of the Cantos of Ezra Pound. It was published well after the second world war but it refers to the period after 1929 when Churchill ceased to be the Chancellor of the Exchequer (not the most glorious period of his career!).

May have let the bacon come home,
                    To watch how they'll slip and slide
                    watch how they'll try to hide
                              the real portent
          To watch a while from the tower
                    where dead flies lie thick over the old charter
          forgotten, oh quite forgotten
          but confirming John's first one,
     and still there if you climb over attic rafters;
to look at the fields; are they tilled?
is the old terrace alive as it might be
with a whole colony
                    if money be free again?
Chesterton's England of has-been and why-not,
or is it all rust, ruin, death duties and mortgages
and the great carriage yard empty
                    and more pictures gone to pay taxes

EZRA POUND
from *Canto LXXX*

On A General Election

The battle's set 'twixt Envy, Greed, and Pride:
Come Conscience, do your duty: choose your side.

W. B. YEATS

A Dead Statesman

I could not dig: I dared not rob:
Therefore I lied to please the mob.
Now all my lies are proved untrue
And I must face the men I slew.
What tale shall serve me here among
Mine angry and defrauded young?

RUDYARD KIPLING

Viscount Demos*

Let me be thankful, God, that I am not
a Labour Leader when his life-work ends,
Who contemplates the coronet he got
By being false to principles and friends;

Who fought for forty years a desperate fight
With words that seared and stung and slew like swords,
And at the end, with victory in sight,
Ate them – a mushroom viscount in the Lords.

WILLIAM KEAN SEYMOUR

Farewell To Democracy

Addressed to a certain drawing-room Socialist and his Friends

From year to year you hunt in packs,
From ear to ear you grin,
Advancing in combined attacks,
You, lacking sense, can do no sin.

You hunt in packs, you have to do so
To persecute the chosen few,
Torpedo the island of Robinson Crusoe,
And crucify a wandering Jew.

You scorn as quacks the brain's physicians,
You swap your prophets for a priest,
You strain to profit politicians,
You ravage beauty for the beast.

*This was written in the twenties. Until 1979 the Labour Party had shared fully in the Honours system, accepting awards from the British Empire Medal to Peerages. In that year the National Executive of the party, though not its leadership, decided to refuse all further honours. Mrs Thatcher decided to revive awards for political service since it was anomalous that this alone among all forms of public activity should not be recognised.

116

In all your actions may we see
Mere cannibals who dine on scalps,
Who longer take at ABC
Than Hannibal took to cross the Alps.

To entertain divine Democracy, and nothing bigger,
Was all your aim, and all your aim askew,
For every time, before you pulled the trigger,
The target took to wing, and out of range it flew.

Unguided, giddy, gadding, Gadarene,
Like quaggas in a quagmire you are stuck:
When soup turns cold it sticks to the tureen,
When fools turn clean the angels stick to muck.

Be kind to animals, and blow your nose,
Blow your own trumpet, be a business man,
Kiss the Pope's toe, and cultivate the rose,
Old Age on the box, and Humbug in the van.

Respect your elders, for your betters feel much better
Without your belly-crawling and your loving greetings,
Get back to the Y.M.C.A. and write a friendly letter
To God and ask him to preside at seven temperance
    meetings.

See, panting you pursue those vast pantechnicons,
Art, Life and Science, and get left behind,
The less he thinks the more a man's neck thickens,
The stomach is inflated by a windy mind.

The last car leaves for heaven. Nothing can permit you
To enter, for the seats are all reserved for us.
This is your worst mistake, the bus will not admit you,
Yet you will not admit that you have missed the bus.

WILLIAM PLOMER

The Song Of The Grunwick Pickets*

Bloody scabs! Bosses' narks!
Niggers out! Long live Marx!
Stuff the blossom on the bough!
Smash the capitalist system now!

Kill the fuzz! Kill the pigs!
What they need is Russian Migs!
Margaret Thatcher is a cow!
Smash the capitalist system now!

Blacklegs out! They shall not pass!
Callaghan can kiss my arse!
Revolution! Long live Mao!
Smash the capitalist system now!

Workers of the world unite!
The Baader-Meinhof gang is right!
So's the I.R.A. – and how!
Smash the capitalist system now!

All together, one, two, three —
WORKERS' SOLIDARITEE!
Buckingham Palace to the plough!
Smash the capitalist system now!

BERNARD LEVIN

*In 1979 the Labour Party decided to bring its official song book up to date and its General Secretary, Ron Hayward, wrote to all its branches asking for suggestions. Bernard Levin composed this parody of a song that he had heard was to be included. The Grunwick factory in North London was the scene in 1977 of violent mass picketing, which was directed at getting the management to recognise a union. Cabinet ministers appeared on the picket line and there were many attacks on the police. The picketing was not successful.

The Great Day

Hurrah for revolution and more cannon-shot!
A beggar upon horseback lashes a beggar on foot.
Hurrah for revolution and cannon come again!
The beggars have changed places, but the lash goes on.

W. B. YEATS

On Jacobinism*

Such is the lib'ral Justice which presides
In these our days, and modern Patriots guides –
Justice, whose blood-stain'd book one sole decree,
One statute fills – 'the People shall be Free.'
Free by what means? – by folly, madness, guilt,
By boundless rapines, blood in oceans spilt;
By confiscation, in whose sweeping toils
The poor man's pittance with the rich man's spoils,
Mix'd in one common mass, are swept away –
To glut the short-liv'd tyrant of the day.
By laws, religion, morals all o'erthrown,
– Rouse then, ye Sov'reign People, claim your own –
The license that enthrals, the truth that blinds,
The wealth that starves you, and the pow'r that grinds.
– So Justice bids – 'twas her enlighten'd doom,
LOUIS, thy head devoted to the tomb –
'Twas Justice claim'd, in the accursed hour,
The fatal forfeit of too lenient pow'r.
Mourn for the Man we may – but for the King –
Freedom, oh! Freedom's such a charming thing. . . .

GEORGE CANNING
from *The Anti-Jacobin*

*This is an extract from a poem in the weekly magazine the *Anti-Jacobin*
that appeared in 1797-1798. This was written by a group of politicians who
detested Jacobinism and all its works. The poems were often written by two
or three people, but this passage is by George Canning, who later became
Prime Minister. He has been the only occupant of No. 10 who wrote verse
successfully.

Private Willis's Song

When all night long a chap remains
   On sentry-go, to chase monotony
He exercises of his brains,
   That is, assuming that he's got any.
Though never nurtured in the lap
   Of luxury, yet I admonish you,
I am an intellectual chap,
   And think of things that would astonish you.
      I often think it's comical – Fal, lal, la, la!
      How Nature always does contrive – Fal, lal, la, la!
        That every boy and every gal
          That's born into the world alive
        Is either a little Liberal
          Or else a little Conservative!
        Fal, lal, la!

When in that House M.P.s divide,
   If they've a brain and cerebellum, too,
They've got to leave that brain outside,
   And vote just as their leaders tell 'em to.
But then the prospect of a lot
   Of dull M.P.s in close proximity,
All thinking for themselves, is what
   No man can face with equanimity.
      Then let's rejoice with loud Fal, lal, la, la!
      That Nature always does contrive – Fal, lal, la, la!
        That every boy and every gal
          That's born into the world alive
        Is either a little Liberal
          Or else a little Conservative!
        Fal, lal, la!

W. S. GILBERT
from *Iolanthe*

On The Left*

The fist-shut Left, so dextrous with the dirk,
The striker, less in battle than from work:
The weed of Life that grows where air is hot
With 'Meetings' for its aspidistral pot:
That leaves its labour to the hammering tongue
And grows, a cactus, out of hot-house dung:
A manual head-ache, fastened in a fist,
And fed with fumes of foul carbonic mist:
A vegetable cramp: a bolted clam
Whose grudging doors on life and daylight slam:
The 'No' to life translated as 'I am,'
A Life-constricting tetanus of fingers
Under whose sign an outworn Age malingers,
While from its back the nails eat slowly through
For communists out-fakir the Hindu,
And hanker for stagnation thrice as vast
Where all must starve beneath the lowest Caste; . . .
Like the raised claw-bunch of an ancient stork:
With cork-screwed fingers, like a crumpled fork,
In a rheumatic ecstasy of hate
Clenched at the world, for being born too late;
This weary fist infests the world entire
As common in the palace as the byre,
As limply fungoid in the idle rich
As when it grimly toadstools from a ditch,
Or, friend to every cause that rots or fails,
Presides in Bloomsbury with tinted nails. . . .

ROY CAMPBELL
from *Flowering Rifle*

*In his long poem *Flowering Rifle*, published in 1939, Campbell sprang to the
defence of Franco and bitterly attacked communism – here his target is the
clenched fist salute of the left. Edith Sitwell liked him and called him "a
typhoon in a beer bottle." Hugh MacDiarmid loathed this poem but he
waited until 1957 after Campbell's death to launch his counter attack in an
even longer poem *The Battle Continues*.

On The Right

The Battle continues.

For the spirit knows no compromise.

But now, if we'd let it (which we won't)
Silence would crack down on Spain with all
The hostile suspicions of a peace conference,
You hope – being always original
As a B.B.C. comedian's gag-book.
Never mind, Campbell, I'll be seeing you one of these days
In the old soldiers' home that Nell Gwynne built
Out of the orange business perhaps.

Men like you in the world today, Campbell,
Are simply human phagocytes
– Wandering cells such as we find
Eating bacteria in the pus of an abscess
Or pullulating in a fissure of the *Anus Mundi,*
With Mosley's Blackshirts, Joyce's National Socialist League,
Arnold Leese's Greyshirts, the Link, the German-American
     Bund,
The National Gentile League, McWilliam's Destiny Party,
Pelley's Silver Shirts, and all the rest.
And your poetry is the sort of stuff one expects
From a mouth living close to a sewer
And smelling like a legacy from Himmler.

Ah, Spain, already your tragic landscapes
And the agony of your War to my mind appear
As tears may come into the eyes of a woman very slowly,
So slowly as to leave them CLEAR!

Campbell, clutch a little longer at the slippery plank
Of your perfidious friends', and your own, praises,
In vain – you will scrabble and plunge into the tank
And drown there in the world's collected *faeces.* . . .

HUGH MacDIARMID
from *The Battle Continues*

Down With Fanatics!

If I had my way with violent men
I'd simmer them in oil,
I'd fill a pot with bitumen
And bring them to the boil.
I execrate the terrorist
And those who harbour him,
And if I weren't a moralist
I'd tear them limb from limb.

Fanatics are an evil breed
Whom decent men should shun;
I'd like to flog them till they bleed,
Yes, every mother's son,
I'd like to tie them to a board
And let them taste the cat,
While giving praise, oh thank the Lord,
That I am not like that.

For we should love the human kind,
As Jesus taught us to,
And those who don't should be struck blind
And beaten black and blue;
I'd like to roast them in a grill
And listen to them shriek,
Then break them on the wheel until
They turned the other cheek.

ROGER WODDIS

We Thought At First,
This Man Is A King For Sure

Addition to Kipling's
'The Dead King (Edward VII.), 1910'

Wisely and well was it said of him, 'Hang it all, he's a
Mixture of Jesus, Apollo, Goliath and Julius Caesar!'
Always he plans as an ever Do-Right-man, never an
    Err-man,
And never a drop of the blood in his beautiful body was
    German.
'God save him,' we said when he lived, but the words now
    sound odd,
For we know that in Heaven above at this moment *he's*
    saving *God*.

MAX BEERBOHM

On Charles II*

In the Isle of Great *Britain* long since famous known,
For breeding the best C[ully] in *Christendom*;
There reigns, and long may he reign and thrive,
The easiest prince and best bred man alive:
Him no ambition moves to seek renown,
Like the *French* fool to wander up and down,
Starving his subjects, hazarding his crown.
Nor are his high desires above his strength,
His scepter and his p.... are of a length,
And she that plays with one may sway the other,
And make him little wiser than his brother.

---

*Rochester was a drinking and whoring companion of the King's, and they
certainly shared one mistress, Mrs Roberts. Charles was very indulgent to
the impudent Rochester. He kept him as a Gentleman of the Bedchamber at a
£1,000 a year when he was virtually bankrupt. Rochester had to leave the
Court when one of his drinking cronies was killed, but he was eventually
forgiven by the King. He showed his gratitude in this vicious portrait.

I hate all monarchs and the thrones they sit on,
From the Hector of *France* to the Cully of *Britain*.
Poor Prince, thy p.... like the buffoons at court,
It governs thee, because it makes thee sport;
Tho' safety, law, religion, life lay on't,
'Twill break through all to it's way to c...
Restless he rolls about from whore to whore,
A merry Monarch, scandalous and poor.
To *Carewell* the most dear of all thy dears,
The sure relief of thy declining Years;
Oft he bewails his fortune and her fate,
To love so well, and to be lov'd so late;
For when in her he settles well his t....
Yet his dull graceless buttocks hang an Arse.
This you'd believe, had I but time to tell you,
The pain it costs to poor laborious *Nelly,*
While she employs hands, fingers, lips and thighs,
E'er she can raise the member she enjoys.

JOHN WILMOT, EARL OF ROCHESTER

On George I*

. . . To quench their lewd fire
They were forced to retire,
Though dinner was scarce down their throats.
But alas! in this hurry,
While with too much fury
The rampant old lecher embraced her,
Her ladyship's weight,
Which we all know is great,
Brought down on 'em both the bed's tester. . . .

ANON

*Compared with the Four Georges, the Stuarts were let off lightly. The
eighteenth century was the greatest period of satire, wit, and caricature in
British history, and the Royal House of Hanover provided some of the best
targets. George I brought over with him two German mistresses and as one
was very fat and one very tall they were dubbed 'the elephant and the
maypole'.

Lovely Albert*

The Turkish war both far and near
   Has played the very deuce then,
And little Al, the royal pal,
   They say has turned a Russian;
Old Aberdeen, as may be seen,
   Looks woeful pale and yellow,
And Old John Bull had his belly full
   Of dirty Russian tallow.

Chorus
   We'll send him home and make him groan,
      Oh, Al! you've played the deuce then;
   The German lad has acted sad
      And turned tail with the Russians. . . .

Last Monday night, all in a fright,
   Al out of bed did tumble,
The German lad was raving mad,
   How he did groan and grumble!
He cried to Vic, 'I've cut my stick:
   To St. Petersburg go right slap.'
When Vic, 'tis said, jumped out of bed,
   And wopped him with her night-cap. . . .

You jolly Turks, now go to work,
   And show the Bear your power.
It is rumoured over Britain's isle
   That A..... is in the Tower;
The postmen some suspicion had,
   And opened the two letters,
'Twas a pity sad the German lad
   Should not have known much better. . . .

ANONYMOUS BROADSIDE

*In the run-up to the Crimean War in 1854 Palmerston, the darling of the masses, resigned. The consort Prince Albert was held to be responsible and accused of being a pawn of the Czar. Wild rumours filled London to the effect that Albert had been accused of treason and was in the Tower. This incident revived the anti-German feeling which had emerged at the time of his marriage.

On George III*

To Whitbread now deign'd Majesty to say,
'Whitbread, are all your horses fond of hay?'

'Yes, please your Majesty,' in humble notes
The brewer answer'd: 'also, Sir, of Oats.
'Another thing my horses too maintains;
'And that, an't please your Majesty, are grains.'

'Grains, grains,' said Majesty, 'to fill their crops?
'Grains, grains? That comes from hops; yes, hops, hops, hops.'

Here was the King, like hounds sometimes, at fault.
    'Sire,' cried the humble brewer, 'give me leave
    'Your sacred Majesty to undeceive:
'Grains, Sire, are never made from hops, but malt.'

'True,' said the cautious monarch with a smile:
'From malt, malt, malt: I meant malt all the while.'
'Yes,' with the sweetest bow, rejoined the brewer,
'An't please your Majesty, you did, I'm sure.'
'Yes,' answered Majesty with quick reply,
'I did, I did, I did, I, I, I, I.'. . .

And now before their sovereign's curious eye,
    Parents and children, fine fat hopeful sprigs,
All snuffing, squinting, grunting, in their sty,
    Appear'd the brewer's tribe of handsome pigs:
On which th' observant man who fills a throne,
Declared the pigs were vastly like *his own*:

    On which the brewer, swallowed up in joys,
    Tears and astonishment in both his eyes,

---

*Peter Pindar was the pseudonym of a Devonshire clergyman Dr John Wolcot. His satirical attacks on George III emphasised his staccato manner of speaking, his attention to trivial detail and his bovine stupidity. Here George III is seen visiting Whitbread's Brewery in Islington.

His soul brimful of sentiments so loyal,
  Exclaimed: 'O Heavens! and can *my* swine
  Be deemed by majesty so fine?
Heavens! can *my* pigs compare, Sire, with pigs royal?'
To which the King assented with a nod:
On which the brewer bowed, and said, 'Good God!'
Then wink'd significant on Miss,
Significant of wonder and of bliss;
  Who, bridling in her chin divine,
Crossed her fair hands, a dear old maid,
And then her lowest curtsey made
  For such high honour done her father's swine. . . .

PETER PINDAR
from *Instructions to a Celebrated Laureat*

*Royal Wedding Gifts**

It is unfortunately understandable enough
That gifts should pour in from all over the earth:
Not so the greed of the girl who accepts so much
And so monstrously overrates her own scant worth.

The daughter of a base and brainless breed
Is given what countless better women sorely need,
But cannot get one ten-millionth part of tho' they slave and
 save
Relentlessly from the cradle to the grave.

Rope in the shameless hussy – let her be
Directed to factory work or domestic service
Along with all the other spivs and drones –
Our life-stream's clogged and fouled with all these damned
 convervas.

HUGH MacDIARMID

*George VI was totally beyond reproach due to the way he had unexpectedly come to the throne and had refused to leave London during the Blitz. The present Queen has not had to suffer the violent and offensive abuse in verse which many of her ancestors had to bear. Indeed the only piece that I have come across is this petulant squib from Hugh McDiarmid on the occasion of her wedding in 1947.

131

Curse*

Curs'd be the Stars which did ordain
Queen Bess a maiden–life should reign;
Married she might have brought an heir,
Nor had we known a S..... here.
Curs'd be the tribe who at *Whitehall*

Slew one o' th' name, and slew not all.
Curs'd be the Second, who took gold
From *France,* and *Britain's* Honour Sold:
But curs'd of all be J.... the last,
The worst of kings, of fools the best,
And doubly cursed be those knaves,
Who out of loyalty would make us slaves,
Curs'd be the clergy who desire
The *French* to bring in *James* the squire,
And save your church so as by fire.

ANON

Ballade Tragique À Double Refrain**

S C E N E: A Room in Windsor Castle   T I M E: The Present

Enter a Lady-in-Waiting and a Lord-in-Waiting

SHE: Slow pass the hours – ah, passing slow!
           My doom is worse than anything
           Conceived by Edgar Allan Poe:
           The Queen is duller than the King.

---

*This is an anonymous 'State Poem' about the Stuarts and James II in particular. However unpopular Charles II became he managed to hang on to his throne until he died, and he was safe from assassination as his heir was his brother James. The latter lost everthing within three years.
**This was written in 1912 about George V and Queen Mary and was supposed to have delayed Beerbohm's knighthood for twenty-seven years.

HE: Lady, your mind is wandering;
You babble what you do not mean.
      Remember, to your heartening,
The King is duller than the Queen.

SHE: No, most emphatically No!
      To one firm–rooted fact I cling
In my now chronic vertigo:
      The Queen is duller than the King.

HE: Lady, you lie. Last evening
I found him with a Rural Dean,
      Talking of district-visiting . . .
The King is duller than the Queen.

SHE: At any rate he doesn't sew!
      You don't see *him* embellishing
Yard after yard of calico . . .
      The Queen is duller than the King.
      Oh to have been an underling
To (say) the Empress Josephine!

HE: Enough of your self-pitying!
The King is duller than the Queen.

SHE *(firmly)*: The Queen is duller than the King.

HE: Death then for you shall have no sting.

      [*Stabs her and, as she falls dead, produces phial
      from breast-pocket of coat.*]

Nevertheless, sweet friend Strychnine,
    [*Drinks*]

The King – is – duller than – the Queen.

      [*Dies in terrible agony.*]

MAX BEERBOHM

133

On George IV*

The foremost of the r.... brood
Who broke his shell and cried for food
Turned out a cock of manners rare,
A fav'rite with the feathered fair. . . .
But though his love was sought by all,
Game, dunghill, bantam, squab and tall,
Among the whole, not one in ten
Could please him like a tough old hen.

ANON

More On George IV**

The RAM turns to this ewe and then turns to that,
Enveloped in pillows, in feathers and fat. . . .
The ladies they played in most excellent style,
And blended their delicate voices the while:

But the old mutton's *flute,* being *shockingly small*
And *very much worn,* didn't join in at all.

ANON

Blue Blood

We thought at first, this man is a king for sure,
Or the branch of a mighty and ancient and famous lineage
– That silly, sulky, illiterate, black-avised boor
Who was hatched by foreign vulgarity under a hedge!

* As George IV got older and fatter he developed a passion for fat mistresses as this lampoon notes.
** In these verses he is not an old cock but a tired old ram. The King wanted the writers of these attacks prosecuted but no action was taken since no jury could be relied upon to convict.

The good men of Clare were drinking his health in a flood,
And gazing, with me, in awe at the princely lad;
And asking each other from what bluest blueness of blood
His daddy was squeezed, and the pa of the da of his dad?

We waited there, gaping and wondering, anxiously,
Until he'd stop eating, and let the glad tidings out;
And the slack-jawed booby proved to the hilt that he
Was lout, son of lout, by old lout, and was da to a lout!

JAMES STEPHENS

War's A Brain-Spattering,
Windpipe-Slitting Art

Verses Written On A Pane Of Glass,
On The Occasion Of A National Thanksgiving
For A Naval Victory

Ye hypocrites! are these your pranks?
To murder men, and gie God thanks!
For shame! Gie o'er – proceed no further –
God won't accept your thanks for murther.

ROBERT BURNS

To Whom It May Concern

I was run over by the truth one day.
Ever since the accident I've walked this way
    So stick my legs in plaster
    Tell me lies about Vietnam.

Heard the alarm clock screaming with pain,
Couldn't find myself so I went back to sleep again
    So fill my ears with silver
    Stick my legs in plaster
    Tell me lies about Vietnam.

Every time I shut my eyes all I see is flames.
Made a marble phone book and I carved all the names
    So coat my eyes with butter
    Fill my ears with silver
    Stick my legs in plaster
    Tell me lies about Vietnam.

I smell something burning, hope it's just my brains.
They're only dropping peppermints and daisy-chains
    So stuff my nose with garlic
    Coat my eyes with butter
    Fill my ears with silver
    Stick my legs in plaster
    Tell me lies about Vietnam.

Where were you at the time of the crime?
Down by the Cenotaph drinking slime
　　So chain my tongue with whisky
　　Stuff my nose with garlic
　　Coat my eyes with butter
　　Fill my ears with silver
　　Stick my legs in plaster
　　Tell me lies about Vietnam.

You put your bombers in, you put your conscience out,
You take the human being and you twist it all about
　　So scrub my skin with women
　　Chain my tongue with whisky
　　Stuff my nose with garlic
　　Coat my eyes with butter
　　Fill my ears with silver
　　Stick my legs in plaster
　　Tell me lies about Vietnam.

ADRIAN MITCHELL

The Boer War

The whip-crack of a Union Jack
In a stiff breeze (the ship will roll),
Deft abracadabra drums
Enchant the patriotic soul –

A grandsire in St James's Street
Sat at the window of his club,
His second son, shot through the throat,
Slid backwards down a slope of scrub,

Gargled his last breaths, one by one by one,
In too much blood, too young to spill,
Died difficultly, drop by drop by drop –
'By your son's courage, sir, we took the hill.'

140

They took the hill (Whose hill? What for?)
But what a climb they left to do!
Out of that bungled, unwise war
An alp of unforgiveness grew.

WILLIAM PLOMER

On Wellington

. . . You are 'the best of cut-throats', do not start –
   The phrase is Shakespeare's, and not misapplied: –
War's a brain-spattering, windpipe-slitting art,
   Unless her cause by right be sanctified.
If you have acted *once* a generous part,
   The world, not the world's master, will decide,
And I shall be delighted to learn who,
Save you and yours, have gained by Waterloo? . . .

LORD BYRON
from Don Juan, Canto Nine

A Death-bed *

'This is the State above the Law.
   The State exists for the State alone.'
(This is a gland at the back of the jaw,
   And an answering lump by the collar-bone.)

*This is a very bitter poem by Kipling on the death of a soldier in hospital. It's a far cry from 'Tommy Atkins' and 'The Absent-Minded Beggar'. After the death of his son John at the Battle of Loos, Kipling became very gloomy about the war and after it he devoted a lot of his spare time to the Imperial War Graves Commission. This poem was written when a rumour was circulating that the Kaiser was dying of cancer of the throat, as his father, the Emperor Frederick, had done. The words of the Kaiser are juxtaposed with the clinical comments of the doctors and a generalised attack on the horrors of the war which the Kaiser caused. The intensity of his hatred is sharpened by the fact that Kipling himself had a morbid fear of dying of cancer.

Some die shouting in gas or fire;
  Some die silent, by shell and shot.
Some die desperate, caught on the wire;
  Some die suddenly. This will not.

'Regis suprema voluntas Lex'
  (It will follow the regular course of – throats.)
Some die pinned by the broken decks,
  Some die sobbing between the boats.

Some die eloquent, pressed to death
  By the sliding trench, as their friends can hear.
Some die wholly in half a breath.
  Some – give trouble for half a year.

'There is neither Evil nor Good in life
  Except as the needs of the State ordain.'
*(Since it is rather too late for the knife,
  All we can do is to mask the pain.)*

Some die saintly in faith and hope –
  One died thus in a prison yard –
Some die broken by rape or the rope;
  Some die easily. This dies hard.

'I will dash to pieces who bar my way.
  Woe to the traitor! Woe to the weak!'
*(Let him write what he wishes to say.
  It tires him out if he tries to speak.)*

Some die quietly. Some abound
  In loud self-pity. Others spread
Bad morale through the cots around . . .
  This is a type that is better dead.

'The war was forced on me by my foes.
  All that I sought was the right to live.'
*(Don't be afraid of a triple dose;
  The pain will neutralize half we give.*

Armistice Day

An ex-soldier remembered that this had been the evening
Of Armistice Day, and one more anniversary was past,
So he stood up and spat on the floor and left the pub
And hobbled off into the streets of slumbering London,
Passing a taxi or two and a policeman on his beat,
And a Rolls-Royce full of bright young people returning
The worse for liquor and a public school education
From a party given by cheerful Jews for harebrained Gentiles.
Boadicea, the cannibal queen, was rampant under Big Ben,
That tribal harridan accused of inventing Imperialism,
And imagine his surprise to catch her soliloquising:

'Go, make the supreme sacrifice of two minutes' silence
Once a year in the midst of your frantic hurly-burly,
Your one-way traffic after the shadows of echoes,
And God will reward you, while you drop large wreaths
(Like conscience-money for the sins of your fathers
And your own feebleness) with an access of smugness –
Armistice Day? Come, I'll cry armistice
To all this mockery. Whole rows of medals tinkle
And mayoral bellies sag as one by one
The captains and the kings are all caught bending
Bareheaded and barefaced, caught red-handed
Making obeisance to one vast mistake.

143

'I remember last year on November the eleventh
How just before the two minutes' silence
A man happened to swallow the wrong way
And was at once seized with a rough bout of coughing.
Nothing could exceed the combined appearance
Of reverence and dismay on the faces of the public
As the man's face deepened from crimson to purple
And bystanders kept clouting his sonorous back:
His tears were as useful as any that were shed there.

'See the poor war-widow, with disabled heart,
With what nice irony she lays a wreath of poppies
Against that futile stump, the Cenotaph –
Flowers of forgetfulness will help her to remember
That memory's an opiate to dull the jagged truth,
And then perhaps in dreams she'll hear the cynic wind
Under the moon bring winter to those garlands, see
The rain bring ruin to the ribbons and wash out
The pencilled epitaph by poverty depressed,
And the sad floral tribute of her hands removed
By morning and the L.C.C.

'Oh take away the marble and the gold,
Cut out the rhetoric, order was not theirs;
Melt all the medals, pour them in the ear
Of sleeping Poverty that dreams of Power;
Go be a bolshevik and live in tenements
Or go to church and quietly serve the state,
You'll see your children raised to hell again;
Banqueting decades hence with artificial limbs
They'll toy with paper poppies and sip obituary hock –'

The veteran heard her, salt tears on his face,
A gibbering ruin of shell-shock and impotence,
And the moon heard her, listening in the mist,
Glimmering on steeples and the sleeping Thames.

WILLIAM PLOMER

The Volunteer's Reply To The Poet*

('Will it be so Again'?)

. . . So the Soldier replied to the Poet,
Oh yes! it will all be the same,
But a bloody sight worse, and you know it
Since you have a hand in the game:
And you'll be the first in the racket
To sell us a similar dope,
Wrapped up in a rosier packet,
But noosed with as cunning a rope.
You coin us the catchwords and phrases
For which to be slaughtered; and then,
While thousands are blasted to blazes,
Sit picking your nose with your pen.
We know what you're bursting to tell us,
By heart. It is all very fine.
We must swallow the Bait that you sell us
And pay for your Hook and your Line.
But his pride for a soldier suffices
Since someone must carry the can;
In war, or depression, or crisis,
It's what you expect of a man

We can die for our faith by the million
And laugh at our bruises and scars,
But hush! for the Poet-Civilian
Is weeping, between the cigars . . .

When my Mrs. the organ is wheeling
And my adenoids wheeze to the sky,
He will publish the hunger I'm feeling
And rake in his cheque with a sigh:

---

*Roy Campbell, who wrote some fine and evocative poems about the
Spanish Civil War and the North African campaign in the Second War,
castigated the soft-faced poets who had done well out of the war.

And when with a trayful of matches
And laces, you hawk in the street,
O comrades, in tatters and patches,
Rejoice! since we're in for a treat:
For when we have died in the gutter
To safeguard his income and state,
Be sure that the Poet will utter
Some beautiful thoughts on our Fate!

ROY CAMPBELL

First World War Poets

You went to the front like sheep
And bleated at the pity of it
In academies that smell of abattoirs
Your poems are still studied

You turned the earth to mud
Yet complain you drowned in it
Your generals were dug in at the rear
Degenerates drunk on brandy and prayer
You *saw* the front – and only bleated
The pity!

You survived
Did you burn your generals' houses?
Loot the new millionaires?
No, you found new excuses
You'd lost an arm or your legs
You sat by the empty fire
And hummed music hall songs

Why did your generals send you away to die?
They saw a Great War coming
Between masters and workers
In their own land
So they herded you over the cliffs to be rid of you
How they hated you while you lived!
How they wept over you once you were dead!

What did you fight for?
A new world?
No – an old world already in ruins!
Your children?
Millions of children died
Because you fought for your enemies
And not against them!

We will not forget!
We will not forgive!

EDWARD BOND

*thanksgiving (1956)**

a monstering horror swallows
this unworld me by you
as the god of our fathers' fathers bows
to a which that walks like a who

but the voice-with-a-smile of democracy
announces night & day
'all poor little peoples that want to be free
just trust in the u s a'

suddenly uprose hungary
and she gave a terrible cry
'no slave's unlife shall murder me
for i will freely die'

---

*The month of October 1956 was one of the most traumatic since the Second
World War. The invasion of Suez was launched and within days the West
was being wrenched apart. The Russians launched their invasion of Hungary
to overthrow the liberal regime of Imre Nagy. The most moving broadcast
I've ever heard was his last appeal for help as the Russian tanks approached
Budapest, an appeal to which the West turned a particularly deaf ear. Nagy
was arrested by the Russians and never heard of since.

she cried so high thermopylae
heard her and marathon
and all prehuman history
and finally The UN

'be quiet little hungary
and do as you are bid
a good kind bear is angary
we fear for the quo pro quid'

uncle sam shrugs his pretty
pink shoulders you know how
and he twitches a liberal titty
and lisps 'i'm busy right now'

so rah-rah-rah democracy
let's all be as thankful as hell
and bury the statue of liberty
(because it begins to smell)

e. e. cummings

The Enlisted Man

Yelled Colonel Corporal Punishment at Private Reasons:
   'Rebels like you have no right to enlist –
Or to exist!'
Major Considerations leered approval,
   Clenching his fist,
   And gave his fierce moustache a fiercer twist.
So no appeal, even to General Conscience,
   Kept Private Reasons' name off the defaulter-list.

ROBERT GRAVES

Christ Goodbye*

Or how we turn Christ into an 'inhuman martyr' in Belfast

I

Dandering home from work at mid
-night, they tripped Him up on a ramp
asked Him if He were a 'Catholic'...

A wee bit soft in the head He was,
the last person in the world you'd want
to hurt:
    His arms and legs, broken,
His genitals roasted with a ship
-yard worker's blow lamp.

II

In all the stories that the Christian Brothers
tell you of Christ He never screamed
like this. Surely this is not the way
to show a 'manly bearing'
screaming for them to PLEASE STOP!
and then, later, like screaming for death!

When they made Him wash the stab
wounds at the sink, they kept on
hammering Him with the pick
-axe handle; then they pulled
Christ's trousers down, threatening to
'cut off His balls'!
    Poor boy Christ, for when
they finally got round to finishing Him off
by shooting Him in the back of the head

'The poor Fenian fucker was already dead!'

PADRAIC FIACC

*Padraic Fiacc was born in Ulster, educated in New York but returned to his native land in 1946. He has also produced an anthology of Ulster poetry *The wearing of the Black* which shows that the tragedy of Ulster has produced some fine poetry that cries out against the hatred and bigotry that has engulfed the people in violence and suffering for over ten years.

Memorial Tablet

Squire nagged and bullied till I went to fight
(Under Lord Derby's scheme). I died in hell –
(They called it Passchendaele); my wound was slight,
And I was hobbling back, and then a shell
Burst slick upon the duck-boards; so I fell
Into the bottomless mud, and lost the light.

In sermon-time, while Squire is in his pew,
He gives my gilded name a thoughtful stare;
For though low down upon the list, I'm there:
'In proud and glorious memory' – that's my due.
Two bleeding years I fought in France for Squire;
I suffered anguish that he's never guessed;
Once I came home on leave and then went west.
What greater glory could a man desire?

SIEGFRIED SASSOON

Come Let Us Mock At The Great

Come Let Us Mock At The Great

Come let us mock at the great
That had such burdens on the mind
And toiled so hard and late
To leave some monument behind,
Nor thought of the levelling wind.

Come let us mock at the wise;
With all those calendars whereon
They fixed old aching eyes,
They never saw how seasons run,
And now but gape at the sun.

Come let us mock at the good
That fancied goodness might be gay,
And sick of solitude
Might proclaim a holiday:
Wind shrieked – and where are they?

Mock mockers after that
That would not lift a hand maybe
To help good, wise or great
To bar that foul storm out, for we
Traffic in mockery. . . .

W. B. YEATS
from *Nineteen hundred and nineteen*

Epitaph For G. B. Shaw *

I strove with all, for all were worth my strife.
    Nature I loathed, and, next to Nature, Art.
I chilled both feet on the thin ice of Life.
    It broke, and I emit one final fart.

MAX BEERBOHM

*The fastidious Beerbohm never published this. The source was Ezra Pound who recited it to a Professor Giovannini when he was an inmate at St. Elizabeth's Hospital in Washington (1945–1958). Pound lived at Rapallo where Beerbohm had taken up residence before the First World War, and he called this Maxie's epitaph.

On Garrick*

. . . Here lies David Garrick, describe him who can,
An abridgment of all that was pleasant in man:
As an actor, confess'd without rival to shine;
As a wit, if not first, in the very first line:
Yet, with talents like these, and an excellent heart,
This man had his failings – a dupe to his art.
Like an ill judging beauty, his colours he spread,
And be-plaster'd with rouge his own natural red.
On the stage he was natural, simple, affecting;
'Twas only that when he was off he was acting.
With no reason on earth to go out of his way,
He turn'd and he varied full ten times a day:
Though secure of our hearts, yet confoundedly sick
If they were not his own by finessing and trick:
He cast off his friends, as a huntsman his pack,
For he knew when he pleased he could whistle them
    back.
Of praise a mere glutton, he swallow'd what came,
And the puff of a dunce he mistook it for fame;
Till his relish grown callous, almost to disease,
Who pepper'd the highest was surest to please.
But let us be candid, and speak out our mind,
If dunces applauded, he paid them in kind...

OLIVER GOLDSMITH
from *Retaliation*

---

*This is Oliver Goldsmith's famous description of the actor David Garrick, who had incurred Goldsmith's anger for composing a couplet over a dinner in St James Coffee House when several of Goldsmith's friends were present:

Here lies poet Goldsmith, for shortness called Noll
Who wrote like an angel, but talked like poor Poll.

This piece is not sustained invective, for Goldsmith's amiable character keeps breaking through to make his attack rather balanced. Nonetheless it contains two piercing and memorable couplets that have been quoted time and time again for other targets by lesser wits.

Gehazi*

Whence comest thou, Gehazi,
   So reverend to behold,
In scarlet and in ermines
   And chain of England's gold?
'From following after Naaman
   To tell him all is well,
Whereby my zeal hath made me
   A Judge in Israel.'

Well done, well done, Gehazi!
   Stretch forth thy ready hand.
Thou barely 'scaped from judgment,
   Take oath to judge the land
Unswayed by gift of money
   Or privy bribe, more base,
Of knowledge which is profit
   In any market-place.

*In this piece of sustained vituperation Kipling combines his latent anti-semitism with his hatred of the slippery politician and the financial speculator. Gehazi was Elisha's servant who deceitfully extracted a reward from Naaman whom Elisha had cured of leprosy. As a punishment Elisha cursed him with Naaman's leprosy.

The target was Sir Rufus Isaacs, whose career had started with him being hammered on the Stock Exchange and ended with his appointment as Viceroy of India. As Attorney General in 1912 he was a leading figure in the Marconi Scandal. Rumours started to spread that government ministers, including Lloyd George and Isaacs, had bought shares in the Marconi company just before an important government contract was issued. Both denied this and took libel actions to defend their names. However they were forced to reveal that they had bought shares in the American Marconi company, not the English one which had got the contract.

Strictly speaking they had told the truth, but they had behaved very foolishly. This scandal did not affect their careers – within three months Isaacs was the Lord Chief Justice and within three years Lloyd George was the Prime Minister. Asquith thought that this was the most painful incident in his life, and Churchill thought the Tories, by being too nice, had lost the chance of bringing down the Government.

Search out and probe, Gehazi,
    As thou of all canst try,
The truthful, well-weighed answer
    That tells the blacker lie –
The loud, uneasy virtue,
    The answer feigned at will,
To overbear a witness
    And make the Court keep still.

Take order now, Gehazi,
    That no man talk aside
In secret with his judges
    The while his case is tried.
Lest he should show them – reason
    To keep a matter hid,
And subtly lead the questions
    Away from what he did.

Thou mirror of uprightness,
    What ails thee at thy vows?
What means the risen whiteness
    Of the skin between thy brows?
The boils that shine and burrow,
    The sores that slough and bleed –

The leprosy of Naaman
    On thee and all thy seed?
        Stand up, stand up, Gehazi,
            Draw close thy robe and go,
        Gehazi, Judge in Israel,
            A leper white as snow!

                            RUDYARD KIPLING

Colloque Imaginaire

(After Verlaine)

'The Duce... set the pace... at such a speed that Herr Hitler had difficulty in keeping up with him.'

'Signor Mussolini arrived in his special train (at Essen) soon after 8 a. m. He was received on the platform by Herr Hitler, whose special train had arrived a quarter of an hour earlier.' – *News items, Sept. 27th (1938)*.

The two dictators, seated cheek by jowl
Converse with smiles more horrid than their scowl.

– You're fatter, Führer, since I saw you last.
– Duce, it was not planned to run so fast.

– You ought to exercise, or ride at least.
Nein, nein! The horse is not a Nordic beast.

– Here is some gargle from my own supplies,
I heard your throat conked out. – Bolshevik lies!

You like my blondes, for racial rapture ripe?
– As cradle-fillers, good; but not my type.

– What will you dine on? Make yourself at home.
– Why, Wienerschnitzel, as it's cooked in Rome!

Is this herd docile, Führer, which I view?
–*Ja!* By my order they are cheering *you*.

The Axis, you have brought it, if you please?
– *Si*. Packed inside my bullet-proof valise.

– The wave of public joy is now rehearsed.
See you at Krupps, *But let me get there first!*

SAGITTARIUS

A Certain Statesman*

The DAILY HERALD
Is unkind.
It has been horrid
About my nice new war.
I shall burn the DAILY HERALD.

I think, myself,
That my new war
Is one of the nicest we've had;
It is not war really,
It is only a training for the next one,
And saves the expense
of Army Manoeuvres.
Besides, we have not declared war;
We are merely restoring order –
As the Germans did in Belgium,
As I hope to do later
In Ireland.
I never really liked
The late Tsar;
He was very weak and reactionary.
He never killed anyone himself;

---

*In 1919 Churchill persuaded the Versailles Conference to intervene in Russia against the revolutionary government of Lenin. Britain supplied tanks and munitions to the White Russians but the Bolshevik Army steadily destroyed them, and by the end of the year the British troops had withdrawn. This was a lost cause if ever there was one, but it appealed to Churchill who had a weakness for the unexpected attack on the unguarded flank.

Osbert Sitwell wrote three poems for the *Daily Herald* which was edited by the veteran socialist, George Lansbury, and they appeared as leaders. Sitwell's dislike of Churchill probably stemmed from the time when his father had rented a house from the Churchill family and the young Osbert had to endure looking at walls covered by pictures of the young Winston. He clearly had in his mind the report of an interview in which Churchill had told Sassoon that 'War was the normal occupation of man,' for Sitwell transposes these words into the poem.

But Koltchak
Is a splendid chap;
If he does not kill people with his own hands
At least he has buried them alive!
No one can call that reaction.
It is a real advance on Tsarism.
When Koltchak
Murders and mutilates
His enemies,
It is justice pure and simple;
Whereas we all know
That the Bolsheviks
Commit atrocities.
I shall burn the DAILY HERALD.

As I said in a great speech
After the last great war,
I begin to fear
That the nation's heroic mood
Is over.
Only three years ago
I was allowed to waste
A million lives in Gallipoli,
But now
They object to my gambling
With a few thousand men
In Russia!
It does seem a shame.
I shall burn the DAILY HERALD.

I consider
That getting killed
Should be
The normal occupation
Of other people.
I enjoyed
Doing my bit in France
Immensely.
And am only sorry
That the war stopped
Before I could go out again.

Perhaps I may go out to Russia
– But it must be
To lead
A really
Big
Retreat;
So far
We have only had
Little ones
Of a hundred miles or so.
Who is more qualified
To lead a retreat
Than the victor
Of Gallipoli, Antwerp, and Sydney Street?
This reminds me
That Peter the Painter
Is said to be in Russia.
I shall enjoy
Defeating him again.
I shall take out
My old fire-brigade with me –
And shall burn the DAILY HERALD.

OSBERT SITWELL

The Mountebank Of Mourne*

Oh, Mary, this Enoch's a wonderful sight,
With his warnings so dark and his cheekbones so white;
His eyes burn with anger like smouldering peat,
But he trembles in terror of losing his seat.

He stirs up the blood, then he makes it run cold
With Acts that are nearly three hundred years old;
But a small, leaking boat's where I'd like him to be,
With a Northern wind bearing him far out to sea.

*Mr Enoch Powell's speech on Catholicism and the Crown was delivered in
Mourne, Co. Down in 1978.

A nose for an issue, one freely admits,
Looks fine on a fellow who lives by his wits;
He's tried immigration, inflation, the lot –
But there's none can compare with a Vatican plot.

The Man-to-be-King should be free to decide
On the depth of his love and the choice of his bride.
Though they'd all of them suffer a fatal attack
If the Prince chose a Protestant bride who was black.

ROGER WODDIS

On The Duke Of Buckingham*

Some of their chiefs were princes of the land:
In the first rank of these did Zimri stand;
A man so various, that he seemed to be
Not one, but all mankind's epitome.
Stiff in opinions, always in the wrong,
Was every thing by starts, and nothing long:
But, in the course of one revolving moon,
Was chymist, fiddler, statesman, and buffoon;
Then all for women, painting, rhyming, drinking;
Besides ten thousand freaks that died in thinking.
Blest madman, who could every hour employ,
With something new to wish, or to enjoy!

*These lines are from one of the most quoted political poems. In 1978 in the space of twelve months both Mr Callaghan and Mrs Thatcher quoted from them in major speeches. Dryden's description has made Buckingham live in the knowledge of the world, although he was not a very important figure. A friend of Charles in the Civil War, he went into exile with him but returned three years before the Restoration to seduce and marry the daughter of the Parliamentary General, Fairfax. He was at the centre of politics but not central. He was the 'B' of the Cabal, but he was duped by both Louis XIV and Charles II over the re-negotiation of the Anglo–French treaty. After being attacked in Parliament over this he was dropped by the King and by the late 1670's was in opposition. This portrait is not unfair. He was a libertine who went through one of the largest fortunes in England, spending £30,000 on his dress for Charles II's coronation. In 1671 a group of friends agreed to run his estates and pay him an allowance.

161

Railing and praising were his usual themes;
And both (to shew his judgment) in extremes:
So over violent, or over civil,
That every man, with him, was God or Devil.
In squandring wealth was his peculiar art:
Nothing went unrewarded, but desert.
Beggared by fools, whom still he found too late,
He had his jest, and they had his estate.
He laughed himself from Court, then sought relief
By forming parties, but could ne'er be chief;
For, spite of him, the weight of business fell
On Absalom and wise Achitophel:
Thus, wicked but in will, of means bereft,
He left not faction, but of that was left…

JOHN DRYDEN
from *Absalom and Achitophel*

*The Lost Leader**

Just for a handful of silver he left us,
    Just for a riband to stick in his coat –
Found the one gift of which fortune bereft us,
    Lost all the others she lets us devote;
They, with the gold to give, doled him out silver,

*Poets who are turncoats get it in the neck from their colleagues. This is
Browning's scathing denunciation of Wordsworth's desertion of the liberal
cause. Part of this poem was quoted to great dramatic effect by Nigel Birch
in 1963 in the debate on the Profumo affair. He was taking revenge on
Harold MacMillan for the way he had received the resignation of himself,
the Chancellor of the Exchequer and Enoch Powell in 1957. MacMillan
referred to this as 'a little local difficulty', and went on an overseas tour.
When Macmillan's back was against the wall over Profumo, Nigel Birch
called for a new leader who could give the Tory Party 'glad confident
morning again.'

So much was theirs who so little allowed;
How all our copper had gone for his service!
　Rags – were they purple, his heart had been proud!
We that had loved him so, followed him, honoured him,
　Lived in his mild and magnificent eye,
Learned his great language, caught his clear accents,
　Made him our pattern to live and to die!
Shakespeare was of us, Milton was for us,
　Burns, Shelley, were with us – they watch from their
　　graves!
He alone breaks from the van and the freemen,
　He alone sinks to the rear and the slaves!

We shall march prospering, – not thro' his presence;
　Songs may inspirit us, – not from his lyre;
Deeds will be done, – while he boasts his quiescence,
　Still bidding crouch whom the rest bade aspire:
Blot out his name, then, record one lost soul more,
　One task more declined, one more footpath untrod,
One more devil's triumph and sorrow for angels,
　One wrong more to man, one more insult to God!
Life's night begins: let him never come back to us!
　There would be doubt, hesitation and pain,
Forced praise on our part – the glimmer of twilight,
　Never glad confident morning again!
Best fight on well, for we taught him, – strike gallantly,
　Menace our heart ere we master his own;
Then let him receive the new knowledge and wait us,
　Pardoned in Heaven, the first by the throne!

ROBERT BROWNING

On Sir John Vanbrugh, Architect

Under this stone, reader, survey
Dead Sir John Vanbrugh's house of clay.
Lie heavy on him, earth! for he
Laid many heavy loads on thee.

ABEL EVANS

On Addison*

. . . Peace to all such! but were there one whose fires
True genius kindles, and fair fame inspires,
Blest with each talent and each art to please,
And born to write, converse, and live with ease:
Shou'd such a man, too fond to rule alone,
Bear, like the *Turk*, no brother near the throne,
View him with scornful, yet with jealous eyes,
And hate for arts that caus'd himself to rise;
Damn with faint praise, assent with civil leer,
And without sneering, teach the rest to sneer;
Willing to wound, and yet afraid to strike,
Just hint a fault, and hesitate dislike;
Alike reserv'd to blame, or to commend,
A tim'rous foe, and a suspicious friend,
Dreading ev'n fools, by flatterers besieg'd,
And so obliging that he ne'er oblig'd;
Like *Cato*, give his little Senate laws,
And sit attentive to his own applause;
While wits and templers ev'ry sentence raise,
And wonder with a foolish face of praise.
Who but must laugh, if such a man there be?
Who would not weep, if *Atticus* were he! . . .

ALEXANDER POPE
from *The Epistle to Dr. Arbuthnot*

*Hugh Kingsmill thought that this was 'the most studied and delicate piece
of invective in the language.' It is certainly the most quoted. Pope's attack
probably arose from Addison's view that the best translation of the *Iliad* was
by Tickell and this view was expressed just before Pope was to publish his
own. Addison had generally encouraged Pope's critics and although they
had been friends, Pope had become conscious of 'a deceptive friendship.'
Never has malice been so economical.

Haiku For Margaretta D'Arcy
On Her Rubbishing Of My Play*

Didn't Lenin sort
You out bloody years ago?
'Childish disorders'

Fanatical mouths
Stink of a vicious belly
Fermenting hatred

You have some courage
Let's acknowledge your courage
It is worthless pain

You want to speak out
You fear hangmen at your throat
Panic and scream lies

You yell for freedom
But your voice rasps with future
Prison doors closing

Bad poets like you
Could kill children of the flats
In brand new H-Blocks

*This poem was written by the playwright Howard Brenton and published
as a letter to the editor following an unfavourable review of his play, *Sore
Throats* in the *New Statesman* by a guest drama critic. She had written: 'There
will certainly be no riot at the Warehouse, with its quotations from Brecht in
the programme; its "Save our Theatre" leaflets on your seat; its new play by
Mr Brenton, a work of closet misogeny if ever there was one, disguised as
Women's Lib (his wife-beating policeman, by whom we are supposed to be
shocked, is given all the most sympathetic and personal speeches); and, to
delight our eyes, its close-up porn-pic of a black woman's gaping vagina
among the litter of the stage set. Theatre workers' acquiescence in such
reactionary contradictions can only be due to careerism, apathy, or fear – all
stock weapons in the armoury of the power-monolith.'

Filth lies on the stage
You say that makes my play filth –
Censors talk like that

For what it is worth
This poet says 'England out
Of Ireland now'

Colonial wars
At the end of Empire's day
Kill for year on year

The one million
Protestants, what, deported?
Gassed? D'Arcy is dumb

D'Arcy's for romance
Romance in socialist thought
Can end up racist

Future Ireland
Is a socialist state or
A filthy graveyard

When the peace breaks out
D'Arcy will want a new war
To kill the lovers

D'Arcy can't forgive
Writers for their gentleness
Because she can't write

Writers understand
Hate cannot amplify truth
Contradiction can

You attack my play
Now I attack your review
Who enlightens whom?

HOWARD BRENTON

To A Sister Of An Enemy Of The Author Who Disapproved of The Playboy*

Lord, confound this surly sister,
Blight her brow with blotch and blister,
Cramp her larynx, lung, and liver,
In her guts a galling give her.

Let her live to earn her dinners
In Mountjoy with seedy sinners:
Lord, this judgment quickly bring,
And I'm your servant, J. M. Synge.

J. M. SYNGE

To Nye Bevan Despite His Change Of Heart

Because I loved him
I believe that somebody dropped blood-freezing powder
Into the water-jug of vodka which Nye Bevan swigged
Before he asked us:
Do you want Britain to go naked to the conference table?

A difficult question.
Whoever saw Britain naked?

* *The Playboy of the Western World* was first performed at the Abbey Theatre Dublin on Saturday, January 26th 1907. It aroused bitter controversy. Synge had displeased Irish nationalists by his realistic and unvarnished portrayal of the grim, dirty and unromantic life of Irish peasants. In the Third Act, booing and hissing broke out when the Playboy said 'What'd I care if you brought me a drift of chosen females in their shifts itself.' Lady Gregory wired W. B. Yeats 'Audience broke up in disorder at the word shift.' On the third night W.B. Yeats addressed the audience himself, saying: 'The country that condescends either to bully or to permit itself to be bullied soon ceases to have any fine qualities. I promise you, we will play on.' At the end of the first week the nationalist newspaper *Sinn Fein* condemned the play as 'a vile and inhuman story told in the foulest language we have ever listened to on a public platform.' Even then the play could only be heard with many police-men – the symbol of English authority – in the theatre, 'as thick as black-berries in September', as one contemporary wrote.

167

Britain bathes behind locked doors
Where even the loofah is subject to the Official Secrets Act.
But surely Britain strips for love-making?
Not necessarily.
An analysis of British sexual response
Proves that most of the United Kingdom's acts of love
Have been undertaken unilaterally.
There have been persistently malicious rumours
From Africa and Asia
That Britain's a habitual rapist
But none of the accusers have alleged
That Britain wore anything less than full dress uniform
With a jangle of medals, bash, bash,
During the alleged violations.

So do you want Britain to go naked to the conference table?
Britain the mixed infant,
Its mouth sullen as it enters its second millenium
Of pot-training.
Britain driven mad by puberty,
Still wearing the uniform of Lord Baden-Powell
(Who was honoured for his services to sexual mania).
Britain laying muffins at the Cenotaph.
Britain, my native archipelago
Entirely constructed of rice pudding.

So do you want Britain to go naked to the conference table?
Yes. Yes Nye, without any clothes at all.
For underneath the welded Carnaby
Spike-studded dogcollar groincrusher boots,
Blood-coloured combinations
And the golfing socks which stink of Suez,
Underneath the Rolls Royce heart
Worn on a sleeve encrusted with royal snot,
Underneath the military straitjacket
From the Dead Meat Boutique –
    Lives
    A body
Of incredibly green beauty.

ADRIAN MITCHELL

AntiChrist, Or The Reunion Of Christendom: An Ode*

'A Bill which has shocked the conscience of every Christian community in Europe', – *Mr F. E. Smith, on the Welsh Disestablishment Bill.*

Are they clinging to their crosses,
                F.E. Smith
Where the Breton boat-fleet tosses,
                Are they, Smith?
Do they, fasting, tramping, bleeding,
  Wait the news from this our city?
Groaning 'That's the Second Reading!'
  Hissing 'There is still Committee!'
If the voice of Cecil falters,
  If McKenna's point has pith,
Do they tremble for their altars?
                Do they, Smith?

Russian peasants round their pope
                Huddled, Smith,
Hear about it all, I hope,
                Don't they, Smith?
In the mountain hamlets clothing
  Peaks beyond Caucasian pales,
Where Establishment means nothing
And they never heard of Wales,
Do they read it all in Hansard
  With a crib to read it with –
'Welsh Tithers: Dr Clifford Answered.'
                Really, Smith?

*This is probably the best piece of political satire in verse this century. It ridicules a phrase of bombastic oratory, which was F. E. Smith's stock-in-trade. This poem will still be read when the details of Smith's life are forgotten – an ironic inversion of fame. But then that's often the way with well-known politicians. Stendhal, rebuked that he had included Metternich in one of his books replied 'I had no intention of portraying Herr von Metternich. I dream that I shall have some success about 1860 or '80. By then there will be little talk of Herr von Metternich. Death causes us to change roles with such people.'

In the lands where Christians were,
                    F. E. Smith,
In the little lands laid bare,
                    Smith, O Smith!
Where the Turkish bands are busy,
    And the Tory name is blessed
Since they hailed the Cross of Dizzy
    On the banners from the West!
Men don't think it half so hard if
    Islam burns their kin and kith,
Since a curate lives in Cardiff
                    Saved by Smith.

It would greatly, I must own,
                    Soothe me, Smith,
If you left this theme alone,
                    Holy Smith!
For your legal cause or civil
    You fight well and get your fee;
For your God or dream or devil
    You will answer, not to me.
Talk about the pews and steeples
    And the cash that goes therewith!
But the souls of Christian peoples...
                    Chuck it, Smith!

G. K. CHESTERTON

O Age Without A Soul

Inexpensive Progress

Encase your legs in nylons,
Bestride your hills with pylons
   O age without a soul:
Away with gentle willows
And all the elmy billows
   That through your valleys roll.

Let's say good-bye to hedges
And roads with grassy edges
   And winding country lanes:
Let all things travel faster
Where motor-car is master
   Till only Speed remains.

Destroy the ancient inn-signs
But strew the roads with tin signs
   'Keep Left,' 'M4,' 'Keep Out!'
Command, instruction, warning,
Repetitive adorning
   The rockeried roundabout;

For every raw obscenity
Must have its small 'amenity',
   Its patch of shaven green,
And hoardings look a wonder
In banks of floribunda
   With floodlights in between.

Leave no old village standing
Which could provide a landing
   For aeroplanes to roar,
But spare such cheap defacements
As huts with shattered casements
   Unlived-in since the war.

Let no provincial High Street
Which might be your or my street
    Look as it used to do,
But let the chain stores place here
Their miles of black glass facia
    And traffic thunder through.

And if there is some scenery,
Some unpretentious greenery,
    Surviving anywhere,
It does not need protecting
For soon we'll be erecting
    A Power Station there.

When all our roads are lighted
By concrete monsters sited
    Like gallows overhead,
Bathed in the yellow vomit
Each monster belches from it,
    We'll know that we are dead.

                    JOHN BETJEMAN

Stupidity Street

I saw with open eyes
Singing birds sweet
Sold in the shops
For the people to eat,
Sold in the shops of
Stupidity Street.

I saw in vision
The worm in the wheat,
And in the shops nothing
For people to eat;
Nothing for sale in
Stupidity Street.

                    RALPH HODGSON

Doggerel By A Senior Citizen

for Robert Lederer

Our earth in 1969
Is not the planet I call mine,
The world, I mean, that gives me strength
To hold off chaos at arm's length.

My Eden landscapes and their climes
Are constructs from Edwardian times,
When bath-rooms took up lots of space,
And, before eating, one said Grace.

The automobile, the aeroplane,
Are useful gadgets, but profane:
The enginry of which I dream
Is moved by water or by steam.

Reason requires that I approve
The light-bulb which I cannot love:
To me more reverence-commanding
A fish-tail burner on the landing.

My family ghosts I fought and routed,
Their values, though, I never doubted:
I thought their Protestant Work-Ethic
Both practical and sympathetic.

When couples played or sang duets,
It was immoral to have debts:
I shall continue till I die
To pay in cash for what I buy.

The Book of Common Prayer we knew
Was that of 1662:
Though with-it sermons may be well,
Liturgical reforms are hell.

175

Sex was, of course – it always is –
The most enticing of mysteries,
But news-stands did not yet supply
Manichaean pornography.

Then Speech was mannerly, an Art,
Like learning not to belch or fart:
I cannot settle which is worse,
The Anti-Novel or Free Verse.

Nor are those Ph.D's my kith,
Who dig the symbol and the myth:
I count myself a man of letters
Who writes, or hopes to, for his betters.

Dare any call Permissiveness
An educational success?
Saner those class-rooms which I sat in,
Compelled to study Greek and Latin.

Though I suspect the term is crap,
If there *is* a Generation Gap,
Who is to blame? Those, old or young,
Who will not learn their Mother-Tongue.

But Love, at least, is not a state
Either *en vogue* or out-of-date,
And I've true friends, I will allow,
To talk and eat with here and now.

Me alienated? Bosh! It's just
As a sworn citizen who must
Skirmish with it that I feel
Most at home with what is Real.

W. H. AUDEN

The Past

People who are always praising the past
And especially the times of faith as best
Ought to go and live in the Middle Ages
And be burnt at the stake as witches and sages.

STEVIE SMITH

Children Of The Ritz

Children of the Ritz,
Children of the Ritz,
Sleek and civilized – fretfully surprised,
Though Mr Molyneux has gowned us
The world is tumbling around us,
Without a sou
What can we do?
We'll soon be begging for a crust,
We can't survive
And keep alive
Without the darling Banker's Trust,
In the lovely gay
Years before the Crash
Mr Cartier
Never asked for cash,
Now shops we patronized are serving us with writs,
What's going to happen to the Children of the Ritz?

We owe Elizabeth Arden
Several thousand pounds,
Though we can't pay
We just blow in
If we're passing that way,
While we're going
On our rounds,
We'll persevere
Till our arteries harden,

Then we shan't much care
Whether our chins
Have a crinkle in them,
Whether our skins
Have a wrinkle here and there,
We shan't much mind
For we shall then have left our dreary lives behind.

Children of the Ritz,
Children of the Ritz,
Vaguely debonair,
Only half aware
That all we've counted on is breaking into bits,
What shall we do,
What's going to happen to
The foolish little Children of the Ritz?

Children of the Ritz,
Children of the Ritz,
Mentally congealed
Lilies of the Field
We say just how we want our quails done,
And then we go and have our nails done,
Each single year
We all appear
At Monte Carlo or at Cannes,
We lie in flocks
Along the rocks
Because we have to get a Tan.
Though we never work,
Though we always play,
Though we always shirk
Things we ought to pay,
Whatever crimes the Proletariat commits
It can't be beastly to the Children of the Ritz....

Children of the Ritz,
Children of the Ritz,
Though our day is past –
Gallant to the last –

Without the wherewithal to live upon our wits.
Please say a prayer
For all the frail and fair
And futile little Children of the Ritz.

NOEL COWARD
from *Words and Music*

Degrees

We are the ones with Fabergé's eggs
concealed about our persons, or walking
humpty-dumpty up the ante-natal clinic path.
No doubt you wish we were not here at all,
gazing out over the heads of sleeping children
at the boxes which are our homes, and gardens
full of prams and strung with washing lines.

We are the ones who don't appear too much,
the ones which modern English poetry
could do without. We don't hold degrees,
except perhaps of feeling, the mercury
shooting up and down like crazy.
Oh lord, the thermometers we break,
the sweaty sheets in which we lie awake!

We have no O levels, or A levels either.
We didn't fight and we didn't win,
we only ran to get the washing in.
Look out, you just missed us
as you crossed the crowded campus.
We were only there to clean the floors
and hand your morning coffee out.

ELIZABETH BARTLETT

Lullaby

Here is the guillotine,
Here its good blade,
Here is the convict,
Here is the judge and,
Here the skilled headsman.
Here is a juror,
    and eleven more
    sensible fellows
    never in court before.

Here is the judgement,
Here is the crime,
Here is the punishment,
    in our God's name
    in your name and mine
    go from the court-house
    into the lime.

Here are three Sundays,
Here is the warden,
Here is God's spokesman,
    and here, beside him,
    the convict's weight
    and how he will die
    gleam like steel
    in the hangman's blue eye.

Here is the frail throat,
Here is the knot
    long as a thumb,
Here is the spring from
Here to eternity
    dressed in a hood.
    And be it a man
    or a woman, they shit
    themselves and they come
    as they swing,

and their necks get as long
as a baby's arm
over the side of a pram,
as the soul goes adrift.

Here is the court-house,
Here is the hangman,
Here he is sleeping,
Here is his candle,
   and the dozen true men
   have provided a daughter
   to comfort his slumber.

CHRISTOPHER LOGUE

The Social Realists

Useless, they lingered on the edge of fate;
Purveying culture to midland cities
Godless and sorry for unworking men.
Slumps they had not caused weighed down their backs.

So in symbols or in fact went North
To the rich barrenness of glacial strands
Or, apologetic for chaotic wrongs,
Vaguely tended the wounds of war-torn Spain
And fussed nervously over extremes of blood.

Cissies on horseback, they did not like the sound of bombs
(And who can blame them?) when paranoic toughs
Blundered through Europe with bullying guns
And spies reported chance words of freedom.
All that they loved was questioned in closed vans
And bludgeoned by ignorant power.
Cultured professors writhed beneath jackboots
Whose undiscerning energies claimed only
The immediate animal's survival.

Later, after panic trips around the world,
Their fears were quieted and they returned
To write propaganda or help with the fire service
Which consecrated a holocaust of civilian deaths.

And in the forties they burgeoned with innocent power.

BRIAN HIGGINS

Epitaph For A Sportsman

His last scrum done, Joe's ready for his God,
Inert once more beneath some massive sod.

LEONARD BARRAS

Prize Giving Speech*

'Mr J. G. Magwort, senior inspector, died suddenly on the
platform while making a speech at a prize-giving at Bendover
School. Our reporter noted that Mr Magwort's speech, after a
normal beginning, became confused and meaningless. This no
doubt was a symptom of the onset of the heart attack from
which he died. The loss of Mr Magwort will be deeply felt in
educational circles. To him is due much of the credit for pro-
gressive trends in education during the past thirty years. Affec-
tionately known as 'Maggie' to his colleagues the late Mr Mag-
wort was a humorist with a fund of droll stories with which he
was always ready to enliven a social gathering . . .'

Thank you for the introduction, headmaster,
Thank you, ladies and gentlemen, members of the committee
So ready to listen to nothing. Good morning, children.
Now I will babble, being an old bald man.
When I came into the hall I was still myself:
Mr J. G. Magwort, a well-paid school inspector
Respected by many, liked by a few,

*This attack on the whole ethos of school prize-giving was written rather
unexpectedly by a New Zealand poet.

Author of a book on Manual Training,
Running like a tram in polished grooves.
Who has unsettled me? What has derailed me?
   I had my speech prepared:
Boys, be alert. Model yourselves
On your chief prefect and cadet captain.
You have nothing to fear as long as you behave,
Work, keep fit, and honour your School.
I even had a little anecdote ready
To prove I was once a young rascal myself:
A little story about catching eels.
Then I looked up, from my chair on the platform,
And saw your absorbed faces, absorbed in private
   knowledge.
Totally incommunicable. I saw too the cherry tree
Planted by your Founder in the green quadrangle
Dropping its feminine petals. Came like a thunderclap
The expectation of my certain death:
Angina Pectoris, a very painful disease.
I heard Miss Higgins, your music mistress,
Fart like a draught mare. I saw myself
As an old ghost, pierced by sunlight, unreal, already damned.
Do not believe us; do not follow us.
Our systems of authority, built for security,
Deceive us into incorrigible vanity.
If virtue cannot, cunning may defend you,
Your dreams of gunmen and black-stockinged girls,
Misery at midnight in the murderous dormitory.
Happy I could be at the end of a black journey
If one of you, or two, even by borstal,
Larceny, sodomy, destruction and revolt,
Could escape the virus concealed in the prize-giver's palm
And defeat our intention to make you like ourselves
Old ghosts and bags of wind, gourds of the Judas tree.
Be reconciled to terror: the night is terrible
In which we move and live and find our being.
Though for me it is late, accept my apology
For having been deceived . . .

                                        JAMES K. BAXTER

183

A Tribute To The Founder

By bluster, graft, and doing people down,
Sam Baines got rich, but, mellowing at last,
Felt that by giving something to the town
He might repair the evils of his past.

His hope was to prevent the local youth
From making the mistakes that he had made:
Choosing expediency instead of truth,
And quitting what was honest for what paid.

A university seemed just the thing,
And that old stately home the very place.
Sam wept with pleasure at its opening.
He died too soon to weep at its disgrace.

Graft is refined among the tea and scones,
Bluster (new style) invokes the public good,
And doing-down gets done in pious tones
Sam often tried to learn, but never could.

KINGSLEY AMIS

Hi!

Hi! handsome hunting man
Fire your little gun.
Bang! Now the animal
Is dead and dumb and done.
Nevermore to peep again, creep again, leap again,
Eat or sleep or drink again, Oh, what fun!

WALTER DE LA MARE

This Is Disgraceful And Abominable

Of all the disgraceful and abominable things
Making animals perform for the amusement of human
   beings is
Utterly disgraceful and abominable.

Animals are animals and have their nature
And that's enough, it is enough, leave it alone.

A disgraceful and abominable thing I saw in a French circus
A performing dog
Raised his back leg when he did not need to
He did not wish to relieve himself, he was made to raise
   his leg.
The people sniggered. Oh how disgraceful and abominable.
Weep for the disgrace, forbid the abomination.

The animals are cruelly trained,
How could patience do it, it would take too long, they are
   cruelly trained.
Lions leap through fire, it is offensive,
Elephants dance, it is offensive
That the dignified elephant should dance for fear of hot
   plates,
The lion leap or be punished.
And how can the animals be quartered or carted except
   cheaply?
Profit lays on the whip of punishment, money heats the
   prodding iron,
Cramps cages. Oh away with it, away with it, it is so
   disgraceful and abominable.
Weep the disgraces. Forbid the abominations.

STEVIE SMITH

Rhymes For The Times

To the Man in the Street

'I don't understand economics.'
My dear man, you haven't to.
Who does? Whoever's responsible
For this mess does less than you!
Simply insist on tip-top living
Is all you've got to do
And get rid in quick succession
Of rulers who fail to give it
Till you find someone who does –
And then do your best to live it!

HUGH MACDIARMID

We Can't Be Too Careful

We can't be too careful
about the British Public.
It gets bigger and bigger
and its perambulator has to get bigger and bigger
and its dummy-teat has to be made bigger and bigger and
    bigger
and the job of changing its diapers gets bigger and bigger and
    bigger and bigger
and the sound of its howling gets bigger and bigger and
    bigger and bigger and bigger
and the feed of pap that we nurses and guardian angels of the
    press have to deal out to it
gets bigger and bigger and bigger and bigger and bigger and
    bigger
yet its belly-ache seems to get bigger too
and soon even God won't be big enough to handle that
    infant

D. H. LAWRENCE

The Latest Decalogue

Thou shalt have one God only; who
Would be at the expense of two?
No graven images may be
Worshipped, except the currency:
Swear not at all; for, for thy curse
Thine enemy is none the worse:
At church on Sunday to attend
Will serve to keep the world thy friend:
Honour thy parents; that is, all
From whom advancement may befall;
Thou shalt not kill; but need'st not strive
Officiously to keep alive:
Do not adultery commit;
Advantage rarely comes of it:
Thou shalt not steal; an empty feat,
When it's so lucrative to cheat:
Bear not false witness; let the lie
Have time on its own wings to fly:
Thou shalt not covet, but tradition
Approves all forms of competition.

ARTHUR HUGH CLOUGH

On Our Modern World

It is a matter of interest to see
How long it is before new inventions
Are put to old uses

Electricity is sent through electrodes
Clipped to the body
Men dangled from helicopters on a rope
By college graduates
Medical syringes used in murder
Men dragged at the back of a car

As Achilles dragged Hector round Troy
But Hector was dead
Power drills have efficiently incapacitated
Blow lamps have stripped skin not paint
Flood lamps illumined
What men should shudder to see by day
I speak only of tools of peace
Not weapons of war

This has nothing to do with you, surely

But your mind is full of modern knowledge
How is it used
In our modern world?

EDWARD BOND

Slough

Come, friendly bombs, and fall on Slough
It isn't fit for humans now,
There isn't grass to graze a cow
    Swarm over, Death!

Come, bombs, and blow to smithereens
Those air-conditioned, bright canteens,
Tinned fruit, tinned meat, tinned milk, tinned beans
    Tinned minds, tinned breath.

Mess up the mess they call a town –
A house for ninety-seven down
And once a week a half-a-crown
    For twenty years,

And get that man with double chin
Who'll always cheat and always win,
Who washes his repulsive skin
    In women's tears,

And smash his desk of polished oak
And smash his hands so used to stroke
And stop his boring dirty joke
    And make him yell.

But spare the bald young clerks who add
The profits of the stinking cad;
It's not their fault that they are mad,
    They've tasted Hell.

It's not their fault they do not know
The birdsong from the radio,
It's not their fault they often go
    To Maidenhead

And talk of sports and makes of cars
In various bogus Tudor bars
And daren't look up and see the stars
    But belch instead.

In labour-saving homes, with care
Their wives frizz out peroxide hair
And dry it in synthetic air
    And paint their nails.

Come, friendly bombs, and fall on Slough
To get it ready for the plough.
The cabbages are coming now:
    The earth exhales.

JOHN BETJEMAN

He Is The Pinprick Master

The Satirist

Who is that man with the handshake? Don't you know;
He is the pinprick master, he can dissect
All your moods and manners, he can discover
A selfish motive for anything – and collect
His royalties as recording angel. No
Reverence here for hero, saint or lover.

Who is that man so deftly filling his pipe
As if creating something? That's the reason:
He is not creative at all, his mind is dry
And bears no blossoms even in the season,
He is an onlooker, a heartless type,
Whose hobby is giving everyone else the lie.

Who is that man with eyes like a lonely dog?
Lonely is right. He knows that he has missed
What others miss unconsciously. Assigned
To a condemned ship he still must keep the log
And so fulfil the premises of his mind
Where large ideals have bred a satirist.

LOUIS MACNEICE

Index Of Poets

Index Of Poets

198

Index Of First Lines

Index Of First Lines

203